THE PRACTICE R℞

DINO WATT
The Relationship Expert

"My father was an orthodontist. In a lot of ways, I felt like I was following in his footsteps. He was a great mentor of mine. I looked up to what he did and how he handled his life and career. I wanted in some ways to be able to emulate that. [Orthodontics] is a second career for me. I chose orthodontics because of the desire to be around people in a positive environment, to make a change, and to enjoy what I do every day.

We go through orthodontic residency and learn how to do orthodontics. Nowhere along those pathways that I followed getting to this point was I taught business. I didn't have a background in business. You can fly by the seat of your pants for a while running a business and you can actually be very successful, but there are so many challenges that come along the way. Until you've really figured out those things and can learn to be a true businessperson, you're going to have some issues. You're going to have frustration; it's going to be challenging.

When I first met Dino, I felt as though I had a successful practice, and yet my personal satisfaction was at an all-time low. Dealing with many frustrations on many levels with how my business was running, how I was able to interact with my employees and was having a very challenging time in my practice.

My experience with consultants is that they come in and try to put a Band-Aid on something. They have very cut-and-dry modes of "Well, this is what you should say, this is what you should do," and it doesn't always work that way. Working with Dino is working much more with a mentor. He is my mentor. He is my coach - he's not a consultant coming in here and putting words in my mouth. He's teaching me how to improve me, as well as my relationships with everyone around me. He's giving me invaluable core business principles that I can build from.

I have experienced an amazing transformation. I think the key concept was narrowing down and creating a very clear vision of what I want, coming up with core principles for my practice by which we can operate by and communicate with each other, and building relationships amongst our team members as well as our patients. It's been really remarkable.

It's made a huge impact on our team, our business, and me."

DAVID DATWYLER
Datwyler Orthodontics

"In this book, Dino helps you restructure your business from your heart. Your team, your clients, even your family will see a shift in not only your company, but you as well. It truly is possible to have a business and not drive yourself into the ground. This book is a must-have to ignite your business success."

-John Lee Dumas, Founder and Host of Entrepreneur on Fire, top-ranked business podcast

"So many business owners overlook the human aspect of their business and focus only on the numbers. However, a business cannot grow without people! Dino recognizes how important the human connection is. As the Relationship Expert, he has made a significant impact on *my* most important relationships, and I'm confident this book will have a powerful effect on yours."

-Leslie Householder, best-selling author of The Jackrabbit Factor and *Portal to Genius*

Published by Our Ripple Effect, Inc.
Salt Lake City, UT
www.DinoWatt.com

Distributed by Our Ripple Effect, Inc.

For ordering information or special discounts for bulk purchases, please contact Our Ripple Effect, Inc. at 4873 Wexford Way South Jordan, UT 84095 801.580.9290

Design and composition by Alysha Thorpe
Cover Design by Rebecca Servos and Scopious Marketing

www.scopiousmarketing.com

Cataloging-in-Publication Data

Watt, Dino.The Practice Rx: The Cure for Inner Office Drama, Politics, Low Morale, the Overworked, Burnt Out, Under-appreciated Owner, and Other Office Ailments / Dino Watt – 1st ed.

Certain names and situations have been changed to protect privacy.

ISBN-13: 978-1515114963 ISBN-10: 1515114961

ACKNOWLEDGEMENT

● ●

What a journey this has been. There is no way I would have been able to complete the goal of writing this book if it was not for the love and support of my amazingly patient wife, Shannon, and the encouragement of our kids. Thank you, Shannon, for allowing me to seclude myself away in my office at all hours of the day and night, help me decide on stories and content structure, and be my cheerleader when I needed the motivation. You are my constant reason to improve myself.

A special thanks to my assistant, Alysha Thorpe, for all of her invaluable help in getting this book completed. Without your tireless work, this book might never have seen the light of day.

A big thank you to my friend Steven Shields for all the hours of research and guidance on this book as well as the CORE program. I'm grateful for the balance your data-driven mind brings to my ADD-driven process.

A thank you to one how is no longer here with us but inspired and encouraged me to write. LuAnn Staheli, you are missed.

Last but not least, thank you to my clients over the last decade, for allowing me into your homes and your businesses. Thank you for your trust, dedication to great relationships, and for teaching me as well.

CONTENTS

FOREWORD

By Garrett Gunderson

First off, I want to congratulate you. Congratulations for investing in you, opening up and reading this book. With a very small investment of money and a decent investment of time, you will see lifetime results. How do I know this?

I have personally known Dino for years. I have even interviewed him for my monthly experts series. I've always liked him. I didn't love him until I went through his program, The Business of Marriage, where he really facilitated a breakthrough in my relationship with my wife. It was so profound that I have now shared the stage with Ariana Huffington, Daymond John, Tim Ferriss, Dean Graziosi, Brendon Burchard and a huge list of others talking specifically about how to create extraordinary relationships. Needless to say, he's left an impact on my life.

Now, in business, relationships can be tough. But in life, marriages seem to be infinitely more emotional and complicated. Dino was instrumental in not only improving our relationship, but in having such profound breakthroughs that the most successful people in the world were asking me, "How did you do it?"

I have worked with organizations that have not-so-great cultures. Most of the employee's time is spent gossiping, undermining, and in fear. They are absolutely no fun to work with. These employees undermine your authority. Hell, and you pay them.

Life is complicated and has enough stress as it is. Why add the unnecessary drama in your office? Well, probably because it just fell into place that way and there was no plan. You are looking for a prescription out of that, and I can tell you that you are in the right place.

Dino knows how to handle the most emotional and difficult situations in the most delicate, yet profound ways. His concepts hit home and will immediately improve areas of your life, leaving you feeling a sense of immediate peace with these insights, even if you only implement one thing.

People are hearing so much about culture these days and are hungry to find books on what to do in order to create the right culture. Finally, I am happy to have a recommendation with this book.

You will learn how to create a specific, powerful vision for your business. This is a rare commodity for businesses, yet it determines value and direction. Far too many companies just let it live on the wall in the form of a mission statement and then die... but Dino shows you how to translate your vision into the hearts and minds of your team, leading to massively positive results and profits.

If you have ever felt inadequate as a manager, overwhelmed as a business owner, or just flat out exhausted, here is the manual to give you a boost of energy, crack the code to eliminate overwhelm, and become a leader rather than a manager.

As a business owner, many questions arise. How do you empower your team or your clients without giving up control? How do you stay the informed leader without having your hands on everything?

What is the actual priority that leads to a better culture, business and satisfied customers or even raving fans? Do you want to design the perfect environment in your office, you know, the one you've dreamt of for so long?

The answers to your questions are in this book.

Dino uses an abundance of examples from successful (and not so successful) offices. You'll love some of the systems other offices have set up, and get a reality check if you relate to the unsuccessful systems. You'll be inspired with new ideas to boost efficiency. You'll spark a new level of passion for your business. You'll sprint to your office in the morning, ready to create systems that are income producing and enjoyable.

It's very important to position yourself as an expert in your industry. Because of this, many of the doctors I work with end up writing a book. Most of them didn't think they could do it initially, let alone know *why* they should in the first place. Dino covers the invaluable benefits of expert positioning, along with other ways to gain authority. On top of it, you'll get great marketing advice to showcase to your community your expert status.

You will end up with a checklist of how to simplify business for your employees and yourself, leading to less frustration and more profit. Dino lays out a demonstration for you to do less and get more - that's something I can stand behind!

In this book, Dino unveils the very code that I have lived by and would attribute my success and happiness to. It is a priority that most all of the world has wrong. It is a game-changer. He nails it. If you get this wrong, it will cost you, and is already costing you big time.

I remember the day I hit NY Times and Inc 500. I found out about both on the same day, yet I didn't plan on celebrating. Dino outlines why not celebrating success is such a damaging mistake. He'll help train your mind to recognize and appreciate the big and small successes you achieve every day, leaving you in a state of abundance and with higher energy.

Congratulations again for picking up this book. Now, invest the time by reading it and diving in head first into the activities. You have the opportunity to create an entirely new office – that one you envisioned before "life happened." Now go make it happen.

— Garrett Gunderson

INTRODUCTION

Thanks for opening this book. I appreciate the fact that you took the time, even if it was only out of curiosity, to crack the cover. We are an "instant gratification" culture; I understand the power of catching your attention within the first 8-10 seconds. So now that I have just about hit that time limit, let me say...

YOU MAY AS WELL FLUSH YOUR MONEY DOWN THE TOILET IF YOU HIRE ANOTHER CONSULTANT BEFORE YOU FINISH THIS BOOK!

That sounds self-serving. I realize that. But my goal actually isn't selfish. It would be if I instead said something like, "Don't hire another consultant before hiring us" or "Hiring my company is the smartest thing you can do for your business."

I want you to finish this book before you hire another consultant so you can:

1. Make the right choice on which consultant will have the *best impact*, and
2. Know whether what they are trying to help you and your team with *actually sticks*.

My real goal is to ensure that *whatever* you do to move the needle forward in your business will *actually work*. The next time you go to a seminar or read a business book, you'll have the tools to make things happen.

I see the same challenge over and over again with business owners. They invest in the typical forms of education while missing an important concept. The intended benefit of the investment is temporary, at best. They might even see a short-term bump in business, but it doesn't convert to growth over the long term.

WHY THIS BOOK IS DIFFERENT

This book is not a collection of good ideas. It's not even a "roadmap" to success that is sometimes left up to your own interpretation on how to get there. This book is a GPS to getting exactly where you want. It will tell you what to do to get from where you are to where you *say* you want to be. When you get off track, and you most likely will, all you have to do is go back to the book and see what step you are missing. Check in on where you turned off the GPS and tried to go out on your own.

There are enough good ideas out there. My goal for you is more than the gaining of knowledge. I want to help you create a hulk-like core to your business. Let's build a business that will outlast employee turnover, client slowdowns and economy fluctuations. Let's get you to the office of your dreams.

This book is not just a collection of some nice information to read then forget in a few months. There are in-depth exercises for you to complete in each chapter. Everything in this book has been thought out and organized so that it can have the highest impact on you and your business in the shortest time possible. Some of the tips and tools are simple to put in place; but some will take more time to complete.

I've knowingly given you some tips that will be hard for you to implement (or to believe actually work) depending on your current belief system, comfort zone and, to be blunt, your stubbornness. I will always back up what I am suggesting with logic, an example and, in some cases, actual numbers from clients.

> There cannot be lasting success in business management without focusing on *relationship management*.

You're currently holding a mini-MBA in the most important areas of your business. You'll gain new ideas and strategies on how to get what you want out of your business and how to give your clients what they want from you.

There cannot be lasting success in business management practices without successful *relationship management* practices in place first.

When I say "relationship management," I am talking about the relationship with yourself, your team and your clients. These three areas are the lubricant to the success of your business. Without that lubricant, you will spend thousands of dollars and countless hours on areas that can never give you the return on investment you're looking for.

Worse than the money and time you spend are the tragic results that happen far to often.

Stress-related health problems, suicide, depression, addiction, divorce, bankruptcy, extra-marital affairs, broken families and all around anger, frustration and distain towards your career.

Looking at the data, the problem is not getting any better. In my humble opinion, it's time to start looking at the results and find out why they're not.

Up to this point, your main source to help you with those challenges has been consultants. You find someone with an idea and experience and have them show you the way. These people have certain techniques to get results in one or two areas of your business. You hire them to help fill in those missing gaps.

This option can be great. It can also be a lot of work and money with minimal results if you don't have your needs laid out beforehand. But before hiring someone, you should know *why* you have your needs in the first place.

A consultant's methods and processes are only as effective as the person executing them. Just because it's a good tool doesn't mean it will achieve the same result in everyone's hands.

A hammer, for example, has a specific purpose—to drive nails into any given surface. Yet, a hammer in *my* hands will produce a different outcome than the same hammer the hands of a master carpenter.

> A consultant's tools, methods and processes are only as effective as the person implementing them.

Here is the secret that the most successful companies know: To get the lasting results you're looking for, results that are unique to you and your business, you have to create an environment, or a culture, that puts the focus back on the *three key relationships*. Once you do that, the systems and processes of running a business become a heck of a lot easier.

I don't have anything against consultants. In fact, your investment in future consultants will be more effective after this book. After you master the concepts in the chapters ahead, you'll have more success *no matter what.*

You must look at the way you have been treating your business and what you are willing to do different. Are you willing to stop blaming and complaining? Are you willing to stop making excuses? Are you ready to make a commitment to better yourself, your team, your business and your family?

Then it is time to rise up and claim the role of the Propreneur!

RISE OF THE PROPRENEUR

When I first coined the term "Propreneur" I defined it as a professional who is now an entrepreneur. If you were a doctor, dentist, orthodontist, chiropractor, or attorney, I'd call you a **Propreneur**.

Most people have embraced the side-preneur, the want-preneur and the mom-preneur. No one has addressed the challenges of the professional entrepreneur. More important, no one has addressed what it means to be a **true** Propreneur.

Before I explain myself, I want give you proper credit for what you have taken on in your life.

You earned a professional degree in law, medicine, dentistry, orthodontics, chiropractic, or another field. Through blood, sweat and tears, you spent thousands of dollars on your education. You learned the ins and outs of your field. Then, you got to a point where you were able to work in your industry. Perhaps after that, you took on more debt and had the guts to open your own business or buy into one.

Only, you did this with little to no **actual** business training. You became an overnight entrepreneur without having ever run a business. I completely honor that drive and enthusiasm. The life of an entrepreneur is not easy and often uncertain. The fact that you took that on after 10 plus years of education says a lot about you and your desire to achieve.

Yet, who actually taught you how to be an entrepreneur?

Seriously, out of all the hours of your required schooling, did you take even *one course* that taught you how to be a great marketer, advertiser, bookkeeper, manager, leader, networker, human resources manager, time management expert, communicator, or a countless other titles that are absolutely required to know to be a successful entrepreneur? Nine times out of ten, the answer I get is no.

Who was it that trained you on how to serve your clients to the best of your ability? What about your ownership of your employees' wants and needs, on top of their personalities, challenges and mood swings? Not to mention their dedication and loyalty to your practice, in-fighting, gossip, hurt feelings and other HR issues?

If that's not enough, you most likely received no instruction on how to integrate your personal, marital and family needs with your business needs.

This is the underlying problem of the professional entrepreneur. I believe it is the root cause of 99% of your stress and overwhelm. It is this on-the-job learning that is causing the death of good men and women, the divorce of what could be happy families and the addiction brought on by not reaching out for help. The problem is that you think you can do it on your own.

A *true* Propreneur recognizes this and decides that in order to be a top level professional, he or she does not need - scratch that - *cannot be* all these roles.

The Propreneur treats their business like a professional athlete. They realize that in order to be a top player, they can only focus on the few things they do best. They must have their mental bandwidth focused on their job to the best of their ability.

The Propreneur prioritizes their life. They are proactive, not reactive, to the needs of their personal health, family time, and marital efforts.

If you ask the Propreneur what the most important thing in their life is, they answer with "my family". You can look at the results in their life and know it's true.

The Propreneur is always investing in new ways to improve all the areas of their life by looking at other successful individuals in their industry, as well as beyond it.

The Propreneur is committed to not follow the crowd, especially if the reason to follow the crowd is based on the excuse, "That's how it has always been done."

The Propreneur spends focused time and effort on his marriage.

The Propreneur controls his or her schedule; the schedule does not control them.

The Propreneur has a clear vision for himself, his family, his practice and what he wants for the world.

The Propreneur doesn't let the typical excuses get in your way to success.

The Propreneur takes chances and if/when he fails, he investigates what went wrong and develops a new plan to move forward.

The Propreneur is fully engaged and present in his personal and professional life.

The Propreneur has no need for escapism from his life, because his life charges him.

The Propreneur has a heightened enthusiasm for his life and what he is creating through his gifts.

Does that sound like the professional you want to be? Even if it's just a simple desire to work towards it, it's enough to get started on the path to the Propreneur.

BRACE FOR PUSHBACK

I do have a warning about change. When you start to change your behaviors and expectations, do not be surprised if some people around you, including your employees and fellow business associates, do not like it. They might even try to convince you that it's a bad idea. For many people, change from what they know is looked at as a threat. People get comfortable with the status quo. Your decision to mess with that comfort level has the potential for some negative pushback.

When you try to grow for the better in your life through new ways of thinking and behavior, one of two things will typically happen to your relationships. Either the people around you recognize it is a good thing and are attracted to the "new you" through various means of support, or they are repelled and want to keep you at the level they are comfortable at through means of sabotage. These forms of sabotage range from complaints to quitting. Do not let this surprise you or detour you from your goal.

I have had offices where over a years time, there was an almost 90% turnover rate. That is a hard pill to swallow. However, every single new person who came on board under the new culture and expectations added tremendous value to the team that had not been there before. The business became a more culture-based environment, the team unity was amazing, and most importantly, the numbers were up financially, and the owner went to work every day with more energy, peace and excitement. That is my ultimate goal for you, too.

Through a small shift in your mindset, a little work, and willingness to get what you really want out of your relationships, you *can* have everything you want in your practice and more.

Now is the time to claim your place in the annals of history by stepping up and deciding to get new, better, faster and more powerful results in all the areas of your life. No longer will you be a slave to stress and overwhelm. Gone are the days of a business that sucks your energy and time from your life and the life of those you love.

If you are ready to be more productive and more proactive in your life then it's time to claim the mantle of the Propreneur.

If you want to find more profit in your business and your relationships then your transformation has already begun.

Become the success you were meant to be and the one your family friends and team members are ready to see. This is a movement that will move on with or without you, but will absolutely benefit tremendously with you.

Rise up, Propreneur.

"Whatever we wanted to do, we wanted to change lives. You can choose whatever profession – that's just a variable. The business concepts are the same. In our minds, you take care of your team members first, and then they will then take care of the client and the patient. We will say that over and over and over again. We've had great success with that.

The biggest shock to me was how I thought orthodontics was going to be the tricky part of running the business, but it was really managing people. The other unfortunate education you get as a doctor is how important you are as a doctor. A downfall for many doctors is that, for the most part, we've never failed. We've been successful all throughout in order to get to where we are. We've relied on ourselves only, so we're very poor delegators and poor communicators. We end up where we're the center of everything and we don't treat people the way we should in order to accomplish the greater goals. You can be successful, but most of the time, it's in spite of yourself.

Quickly, you make the association that the patients pay the bills. Many times, doctors will really foster that relationship and treat their patients really, really good, but then they'll minimize their team - call them staff, not treat them well, shortchange them, be cheap and petty with them, and the integrity doesn't run through. The authenticity of it isn't there. It's a big problem.

Dr. Dana Fender said, 'I really like the relationship I have with my clients, but what I love is the relationship with my team.' When he said that, it hit me. I thought, 'That's exactly what we're about.' As a doctor, when you minimize your importance and your bottlenecking of all decisions and everything, then you allow others to rise up and develop personally and professionally. Things go so much better, and your stress as a doctor goes way down."

Scott and Jessica Law

Smile Doctors

THE PRACTICE RX: DESCRIBING THE SYMPTOMS

Over time in my consultancy work, as I dove deeper into the wants and needs of my clients, I've seen that most practice owners suffer many of the same ailments. Here are just a few challenges I hear about from my clients. See if you can relate:

- Employees who gossip, complain or sabotage one another.
- Customers who are not active participants in their own treatment.
- Employees that lack motivation and team cooperation, who constantly bring personal issues into the workplace or create team divisiveness.
- Employees who treat their positions as if they have tenure or are just there to collect a paycheck – they're there to do their job and nothing more.
- Clients who either consistently arrive late or end up not showing up for appointments.
- A spouse who is upset about the way you are running your business.
- Employees who have to be continually re-told how to implement or perform a task.
- Family members who complain about how much time you spend in the office.

- Personal leadership challenges, including motivation, organization, networking, competition, compensation, missing feelings of personal fulfillment and satisfaction, lack of excitement for the profession, and emasculation — the nagging feeling that the team is overpowering any attempt at leadership.

If you can relate to any of the above challenges, you are not alone.

In my work as The Relationship Expert, I have created a practice centered on helping the marriages of high-end entrepreneurs, primarily those in the health care industry. Although I typically focus on their marriage issues, challenges in the practice often come up in our conversations.

The connection between the challenges in marriage and business are obvious to me, but not always to my clients. So in an effort to more fully understand my clients' wants and needs, I began to conduct some private research in the form of interviews of both my clients and other professionals I know. After a bit of research I quickly recognized that most of these professionals were experiencing the same challenges. Those complaints above are all variations of the same underlying problem.

After talking with one of my clients about these findings, as a personal experiment, he decided to send out a text message to 52 professional practice owners (chiropractors, orthodontists, dentists and doctors), asking them to answer one simple question. The question was: "What are the biggest challenges you face in running your practice?"

Like my findings, the responses sent to him had very common themes, but he had a bit of inside knowledge - he had personal knowledge about the current success status of each professional. So the answers could be categorized based upon whether or not the practice was successful or struggling. Those struggling financially overwhelmingly stated that their challenges dealt with employees, patients, money, competition, overhead and insurance. The challenges of the successful practices, however, were based upon education, time to work on the practice, new opportunities, marketing and new streams of income.

Do you see the difference? The struggling practices' answers are based upon challenges with the culture of whom they have hired, who they serve and things that are not in their control. Compare that to the successful professionals who focus on growth, how to be better business owners and other issues that they have a direct effect on.

Intelligent business owners tend to focus on the things they can control, such as their vision, culture, the employment of a complementary team, education, and how to create a movement of clients that leads to referrals.

This book is the prescription to all your private practice needs because it deals with the underlying causes that ails your practice, not just the symptoms. You might think the problems with your practice are the staff, the competition, your clients or even the health care system... but you would be incorrect.

All of those things can be dramatically shifted for the better when you focus on creating a culture of success. When you do, it will act as a magnet, attracting the best team members, clients and reputation.

MY STORY: THE DEVELOPMENT OF THE PRACTICE RX

I have always had an entrepreneurial spirit. As I grew up in the small southern California town of Hesperia, I watched as my parents (a stay-at-home mom and a police officer) tried their hand at multiple entrepreneurial endeavors. From an in-home vacuum installation business to building spec homes and running a craft store, my parents always had a side project in the works. Add this to my undiagnosed dyslexia and ADD (I grew up in the 80s and 90s, when it was just known as "unfocused"). The idea of having my own business and controlling my own time was always appealing to me.

While trying to find what I wanted to do, I worked for major companies like Disney, Nordstrom, Cinemark and Universal Studios. The entertainment world was a big draw for me, but unfortunately it doesn't always lend itself to total control of income. So in 2004, a friend informed me of the wonders of real estate investing and I saw an opportunity.

After two years, my wife and I had found some success as investors. I decided to teach what I had learned by becoming a coach and mentor. I quickly discovered something about couples that work together that I did not anticipate - many cannot work together, and some (really) shouldn't.

My married clients were excited about their new real estate endeavors and wanted to learn, but when it came down to it, they just did not have the skills to work well together in business. Their struggles weren't due to lack of intelligence or their investment in the wrong type of business - it was because they didn't have the right systems in place to balance their lives.

It's challenging enough starting any business. Factor in two different personalities that are just fine when balancing a typical home life, but clash on the business side of things. When it comes to who is in charge of marketing, who the lead decision maker should be, who's going to what networking meeting, what subcontractors should be hired and the thousands of different decisions that need to be made in a business, it can be a bit of a struggle. It has the potential to cause major tension in a marriage.

This dynamic is also different (and more extreme) because a couple naturally feels that they can let many of the business social niceties go; they don't consider or treat each other as co-workers. The emotions of the home and personal environment directly cross over to the work environment, and vice versa.

Because of this, I would often find myself using up 90% of my 45-minute call dealing with marital issues, rather than helping couples with their real estate strategies.

I decided to develop systems to help people work together as a couple. The systems were simple, and gleaned off what I had learned at Disney University, Nordstrom and other companies, both big and small, with my own "marital twist."

One day while talking with one of my client couples, the husband said to me, "You know, these systems you gave us are working really well for us in our business, but they are also helping us in our marriage. Do you teach something like this for marriage?"

That is when the proverbial light bulb came on.

McDonald's, Nike, Disney, Google, or Apple have achieved success, because they have certain systems put into place that they practiced every day. Wouldn't that same success happen if you apply these principles in a marriage?

I realized if I could help couples put similar systems of success in their marriage, they would get a specific result. For example, if successful companies know that having a daily team meeting results in more team unity amongst employees, wouldn't it follow that having a daily meeting in your marriage results in less miscommunication between you and your spouse?

If an employee evaluation or productivity overview once a month in a business results in more engaged and productive employees, wouldn't a monthly meeting with your spouse result in more clarity and a feeling of progression in your marriage?

I started to create systems for all types of the typical marital stresses.

If you are experiencing bad communication, if you are not connecting sexually, or if you are not communicating well about money, systems can be put into place to overcome those issues and get an almost-guaranteed result.

The business was a huge success. No one was mentoring couples this way. Couples who had tried counseling and therapy with no lasting results joined my program and saw huge improvements. Couples who were once on the brink of divorce (one of whom had literally paid the deposit for the divorce lawyers) had a new way to talk to each other. With that came new hope and, finally, a stronger marriage.

The local New York Times bestselling author, Garrett Gunderson, heard about my approach and hired me to help him have a stronger, more powerful marriage.

He had a multi-million dollar business. He believed that one of the ways he achieved his success was by always seeking the best advice through coaches and mentors who could show him a faster, better way and see the things he could not. He is a strong believer that the best way to improve on anything is to hire a coach or mentor as a guide to achieve specific goals.

Just like hiring a personal trainer to help you work out more effectively, or hiring a chef to help you eat better, why not hire someone who can help you in your personal relationships, including your marriage?

Garrett hired me to help his marriage, and he and his wife created great results together.

Because of those results, he started referring me to some of his clients who happened to be higher income entrepreneurs mostly consisting of chiropractors, dentists and orthodontists. As professionals in the medical world, procedures are their forte. When I talked of systems and tools for their marriages, they understood the concepts quickly.

Chiropractors understand that if you want to adjust area "A", you need to make sure area "B" is in alignment. A dentist performing a root canal knows there are steps 1, 2, 3, 4, and 5 to go through in order to complete the procedure.

The concept of systems and putting them into their relationships wasn't that difficult, and success followed.

I started to focus my practice primarily on the propreneurs, and I quickly became the guy to call for professional help with a marriage.

Then, around mid-2012, my "full circle moment" happened. I was on a call with a client who had a very successful dental office, and he said, "Dino, these programs and systems are working great in our marriage. However, I've been using some of the things we've talked about in the communication with the women in my office, and it's actually helping there, too. Do you have a program for my 'other marriage' — my office?"

Once again, that light bulb flipped on.

An office is like a second marriage, with a family dynamic unlike any other.

The more I focused on it, the more I knew I could help business owners create more harmony, happiness and positivity in their offices. The key difference would be the aspect of dealing with multiple people, all with unique personalities.

I realized that in order to get the positive results they were longing for, I would have to help them learn how to first create a *culture* of success, then get the right *operations* in place, strengthen the *relationships* they already had, cultivate new ones, and take that business to the next level through *excellence*.

When Culture + Operations + Relationships + Excellence are used as the framework to your business practices, you have:

The CORE.

With that simple formula, I could help private practice owners create the productivity, positivity and profit they are looking for. That is what I will help you accomplish throughout this book.

WHAT IS THE CORE?

The CORE starts with the most important part of any business: *Culture*.

Culture consists of the vision you have for your business, the expectations from your employees, and the support you are willing to give your employees, because they have bought into your vision and understand the expectations.

If you are a fan of **Good to Great**, the popular book by Jim Collins, you will recognize that this order of culture first is in opposition to his assertion that you must first focus on "who" (hiring the right people), then "what" (your vision for the company). While I do agree with Mr. Collins that having the right people in your business is crucial, most of you already have people on "the bus" as Mr. Collins would say. Starting with the "who" is probably a bit more of a challenge right now. The bus, in essence, has already left the station.

However, I do believe you can still find or create those "right" people once you know what the "right" people look like for your business. The fastest way to do that is to first have an idea of what you want them to help you create through your vision and culture, then develop a blueprint of what those people's standards, characteristics and abilities have to be in order to create that vision with your core values.

In the Culture section, we will help you create your vision and expectations (core values) that will help you decide if the current members of your team are the people you want, or if it's time to start looking for new people.

The next part of the core is *Operations*. The natural thought pattern when it comes to operations is to focus on the flow of things or the sequence, but correct systems and flow in an office is actually a result you get from hiring correctly.

In order to have the right people in place as a part of your team, it's imperative that you hire for passion and drive, not just ability. I will show you how to focus on people's "*Why*" when hiring. We want people working in positions in the office who are working from their core passion - from a place that **excites** them. A mindset that makes them want to do their best, not because they are gaining a paycheck, but because it is their "*Why*" in life. Their core value system, their core desires, and their core wants align with yours. When you do that, you will have the winning team you need.

After you hire correctly, then we turn our attention to systems. What systems are in place for operations to work smoothly and effortlessly? Your systems are essential for a great customer experience. From your initial marketing peace to the closing of a sale, your systems need to create an experience that separates you from your fellow practitioners.

Following that, one of the biggest challenges for many professionals is how to understand their specific responsibilities. You'll come to the realization that you're doing things that are eating up your precious time. This section will help you understand not only the power of delegation, but also the danger of abdication.

I'll then take you into a deep understanding of your *Relationships*.

I feel strongly that the relationships we have in our lives are the most important commodity we have. The first area we'll focus on is your inner-circle personal relationships - starting with you, and then reaching out to your spouse, your family, your friends, and so on.

The second area we will discuss is your relationship with your team. Strengthening this area will give you an incredible ROI.

Last in this section, we'll discuss your relationship with clients. When you focus on these relationships, you can dramatically reduce your marketing budget while increasing your bottom line.

Upon completion of the **Relationships** section, you will know how to prioritize the relationships in your life for maximum benefit.

As we wrap up the CORE concepts, I'll show you how to achieve true **Excellence**. What you learn will answer the question *"How do I take what I have right now to the next level?"*

From understanding the importance of mentors, to encouraging continual education, to celebrating success, the concepts you will learn will set your company apart from your so-called "competition."

The truth? *Your business is only as strong as your weakest link.* In your office, the one "staff" member who's causing the most grief, has the most drama, is continually late, is always asking for a day off, and who always comes up in conversation as a source of struggle, is holding your entire team back.

Your business is only as strong as your weakest link.

As you read this book, you might realize that some people in your office no longer fit into your vision. Some of those people might be employees who have been with you a long time. Some might even have been with the company before you got there.

No matter the circumstances, if you want a healthy office that thrives, you might have to let someone go, and you have to be a good enough leader to make that decision. (If you're worried about this, stop. Don't worry. We will walk through the steps later.)

Sometimes you have to learn how to (as one of my most successful clients would say), "Love them into another job."

In my experience, as you implement these concepts and start creating an office based upon your vision and values, one of two things happen. People either opt out of the "new you" and quit, or they will embrace the change and become part of your new, amazing culture.

My goal with this book is to help you create a hulk-like CORE for your business that will outlast employee turnover, client slowdowns and economy fluctuations, leading you to the office of your dreams.

It's important to note that most of my examples in this book are both from and for chiropractors, doctors, orthodontists, dentists, and other high-end professionals that I work with. I'll also pull from larger companies like Apple, Zappos, Disneyland and Nordstrom. Do not let specific examples discount the ways that these ideas, proven strategies and systems can help you in your specific business, whether big or small, brand new or well-established, struggling or successful. This book will help you to create a core that will be stronger, more *profitable*, more *productive* and more *positive* than you ever thought possible.

YOU MUST CHOOSE TO BE A LEADER

Before we focus on the CORE solution, we need to get your head and your heart in the game. You must be willing to challenge your thoughts and beliefs in who you are and what you can do. You also must believe that you can lead the people you influence toward a better tomorrow.

Let's start where every result in your life and every result you will have started — your thoughts.

To reach the results you desire in your business, you are going to have to make a few changes in the way you think. Within this book are the basic answers to all of your practice's challenges. However, the one thing that will stop you from getting the results you want, no matter the time and the effort, is the one thing that stops everyone from getting results in life — thoughts.

Let me give you an example. A computer system is made up of three general components. There's the hardware, the operating system and the software. Which of these three parts is the most important part in getting the best outcome?

Let me make it more personal. If you were to compare yourself to a computer, you also have hardware. We call it the body. Your brain is the operating system and your thoughts, emotions and feelings are the software. Now, what is the most important part when it comes to getting the success you want? The answer is your software, or your thoughts and emotions.

If you had the best hardware in the world, and the most up-to-date operating system money could buy, but your software had a virus, you couldn't get the correct calculations or output because the software is corrupt. The same goes for you. If your thoughts are in the realm of "I'm not good enough," "I'm a failure," or other disempowering or negative thoughts, your results will automatically be corrupt.

An often referred-to formula when it comes to your thoughts, and ultimately your results is:

THOUGHTS + FEELINGS + ACTION = RESULTS

What you think becomes the way you feel, which becomes an action, ultimately creating your results. Change your thoughts to positive ones and the end result will be positive. Notice I did not say to "try on" a positive thought. Many people just try something only to find themselves reverting back to old habits a short time later. Then, they claim it didn't work because they "tried it out." If you truly want to change your results, you must *commit* to changing your thoughts from here on out. In the Relationship section, you will learn more specific steps to help you have a greater belief in yourself.

Your belief in yourself is the most important part of this entire experience. I cannot stress this enough. Unless you are willing to change your mindset and your belief that you are capable of having a different outcome, no amount of amazing, proven strategies from anyone will make a difference.

Even if you "try it out" for a few months and see some results, unless you change your brain (or the thoughts contained in it) first, those results will only be temporary. Why? Because you cannot get a good result when your software has a virus, no matter how good the operating system is.

Now, turn the attention to your heart. In the first section of the CORE, we will establish your vision for your business. You may have heard this before: "Without vision, your people will perish." Although this sounds dramatic, I do believe that without a good vision, your practice will fail. Owners without the heart of a leader lead to failure as well. When you have the right mindset and the right heart-set (I know that's not a word), you will be unstoppable.

As we have established, no one taught you how to run a business in your schooling, let alone how to be a leader. In order to really have the practice you want, if you have any chance at all to have more energy, passion and love for what you do every day with the people you do it for, you have to be a better leader — even more so, a leader who leads from the heart.

That is not a *"that would be nice"* statement. It's a fact! Why? Because your team, your clients, your family and your colleges need you to be. They are waiting for you to step up and take charge so that they too can be inspired, energized and excited about their lives.

That's right. Like it or not, when you decided to step out into the unknown and be a business owner and entrepreneur, you took on a responsibility that has the power to inspire everyone you come in contact with. As the owner of a business, you have done something most people don't have the guts to do. You took the leap and exercised faith in the idea that people would come to you for a service that can change their lives.

Because of your bravery, your employees have followed you on a journey into the unknown. They trust that you will work hard enough and be wise enough to guide them to a destination every day that will ensure they can provide for their families. Your family puts their faith in the idea that you will care and provide for them based on an idea, a risk, a hope that you can secure their wants, desires, dreams and future security.

So what does it take? What do great leaders focus on that mediocre leaders don't?

The first and most important quality is one that often goes unmentioned and might seem obvious, yet I'd bet that no one has actually asked it of you before. So, for the sake of being thorough, I'll ask it of you now.

Will you be a leader?

It's a serious question and one that demands your answer before you try to implement anything else you learn in this book. The first and most important decision you have to make is to actually choose to be a leader. Are you willing? Do you understand what an affirmative answer to that question means?

The fact is not everyone is cut out to lead... and that is okay. Be willing to recognize your weakness and hire out the leadership if necessary. However, if you are going to make the decision to be a leader, then you must also decide that you are willing to do more than you ask from those who follow you.

In the book *A Curious Mind: The Secret to a Bigger Life*, author and television and movie producer Brian Grazer recalls a time where he had to ask this question of someone who, at the time, was not used to being questioned or challenged in his commitment. He was producing the movie *Far and Away*, starring Tom Cruise and Nicole Kidman. The film is an epic story of two young Irish immigrants in the early 1900s.

The budget for the movie was very tight and Universal Studios expressed concern about being able to bring the movie in on time and on budget. Although Mr. Grazer was the producer and technically the boss on the film, he knew he had to find someone who would accept the role of leader on the set. He could have gone to the various departments and ask them to tighten their belts. He could come on to the set and try to get everyone's cooperation by demanding more form them, even making threats. Instead, he decided to go a different route.

He approached Tom Cruise, the star of the movie. Sitting with Tom, he explained the situation. He also explained that as one of the most successful stars in Hollywood, it was not his responsibility to do more than what he had been hired to do, which was to simply act in the movie.

He looked at Tom and asked if he was willing to help him out and be more than the star and be the leader. Would he lead by example and set the pace for everyone else on the set so they could be sure to get the movie finished on time and on budget? Tom Cruise said, "I am 100% that guy."

He continued, "When I go to the bathroom, I will run to my trailer and run back to the set. I will always be on time. I will be the guy that everyone else will look at to set the pace."

In that moment, Tom fully understood what it meant to choose to be a leader. He didn't just give lip service; he understood what was at stake and what being an authentic leader means. He did not say that he would demand that everyone else run to the bathroom and back, he said he would do it and let them see his example. Just like Mr. Cruise, you are being presented with a choice.

You also have to be willing to be *100%* that person. You have to be willing to set the pace, to do what you ask and not just dictate what you want. If you want your team to show up to work on time, you have to show up early. If you want them to grow in their education, you have to be willing to do the same. If you want them to not gossip, cause drama or bring their home life challenges into the work place, you have to decide to speak positively of others, live a life of integrity and strengthen your home relationships.

Are you ready and willing to take that leadership mantle with all you've got? If not, do yourself and your employees a favor, stop right now and get a job working for someone who is willing to do so.

However, if you are still reading this, I am going to assume you're willing to see your responsibility in a different light than before. You have decided to forge a different path regardless of the setbacks, roadblocks and challenges you've faced in the past. You are ready to be a better leader.

Now that you have made the most important decision, let's take a look at other traits that can help you accomplish your leadership goals:

- **Be willing to be an innovator.** Following the crowd never made anyone a leader.

- **Focus on (and learn from) failure.** The phrase "failure is not an option" is a non-productive way of running a business. Failure is your greatest tool in learning how to be a success.

- **Make quick decisions.** Know you can change your mind later if need be.

- **Be open and honest.** People admire and want to follow those who can admit to their own flaws, mistakes and challenges.

- **Listen to learn, not to answer.** When people know you really are listening to them, and not just waiting for them to stop talking so that you can speak, they feel appreciated.

- **Ask for help.** Great leaders ask for insight and ideas from as many sources as they can find.

- **Generate a positive attitude.** The people you want to be around want to be around positive people.

- **Develop humility.** Knowing that every person you come in contact with is a genius at something you are not, and that you are a genius at something that they are not keeps you humble.

- **Be curious.** Always be looking for a new way, new idea and new possibility to reach your goals.

These are just a few of the important qualities you will need to either develop or strengthen in order to get the results you want in your business. Of course, there are very public and famous examples of leaders who possess these qualities like Richard Branson, Oprah Winfrey, Steve Jobs, and Bill Gates; yet, it's important to look around for examples you would like to emulate in your own field. Who are the practitioners and business owners in your profession that are standing out and making a real difference? Look at what they are doing and follow their lead.

PART ONE

Culture

CULTURE

● ●

"Brand culture and pipeline are the only competitive advantages you will have in the long run. Everything else can and will be copied."

— Tony Hsieh, CEO of Zappos.com

Every few years, a new buzzword or phrase comes along that becomes part of the business zeitgeist. "Synergy," "Paradigm Shift," "Results-driven," "Streamline," "Bandwidth," "Outside the Box," "Touch Points" and many others are thrown around by talking heads, authors and other experts throughout the pages of popular business books and interviews on MSNBC, FOX Business, and CNN. Corporate buzzwords have been used throughout the years to both sound impressive and communicate specific points. The truth is that most of them are just rehashed ways of saying the same thing.

The word "culture" as part of the business world has been around since the 1960s when Carnegie Mellon professor, Edgar Schein coined the term "organizational culture."

Professor Schein's hypothesis on workplace culture: If you create a working environment with an emphasis on caring about the lives, wants and needs of your workforce, will they work more efficiently for you? Could creating an environment of trust and belief in the good of your employees make them want to produce more for you without the need to monitor them all the time?

It sounds basic now, but at the time it was a groundbreaking way to approach business ownership. This new way of looking at a business was revolutionary, and it changed the landscape of the workplace.

The focus on the word "culture" has seen a recent resurgence in the corporate world. Since 2008, new and established businesses alike have been putting an emphasis on creating a culture that differentiates them from other companies.

2008 was an interesting year for the world. We had just started to see the real effects of a crashing economy. Due to the Wall Street scandals, mistrust of corporations was at an all-time high. If you were in business, you needed to find a way to connect with your clients and your employees that would make you stand out without resembling those "evil" corporations. You needed something that made you different but brought people together at the same time. Companies were scrambling to differentiate themselves in the public eye.

2008 was also the year a little book called *Tribes* by Seth Godin came out. In this book, Godin shows the power of creating a group of people around you that think similarly and that have related goals. When you create this culture of like-minded individuals, the path to success can be clear-cut. He argues that as a business owner, you have the responsibility to lead your new tribe by creating a culture where people can easily consume what you have to offer. In turn, they will organically promote your company to others.

Godin explains how, with the World Wide Web at your fingertips, you can choose (from anywhere in the world) who you want to associate with on a daily basis, who you want to do business with, and that the resulting groups can create their own community, economy, and culture.

Both Professor Schein and Mr. Godin introduced these ideas of creating a culture at a time when a major shift was happening in the world. Business professionals were looking for new ways to connect with their employees and customers.

When you think about the word "culture", in terms of your business, what comes to mind? What is your culture? If you were to ask your employees, what would they say it was? What about a client?

Would the responses be *consistent*? Would they be *specific*?

As the owner, you have to choose what culture you want and then create it.

The challenge for many of you is that you have already created a culture you do not want.

You have created a culture of employees who bring outside drama into the workplace. A culture where the politics of the office runs productivity, where your clients show up late or drop in when they want to instead of calling ahead... the list goes on. Most of the challenges you are dealing with in your office are due to the culture that was created by default, rather than deliberate desire.

Let me give you a simple example. (This is a very common way offices create negative cultures with patients, by the way. I see it happen all the time.)

A patient is 15 minutes late for an appointment. He arrives, comes up to the desk to check in and says, "I'm sorry for being late, the traffic was horrible."

The receptionist then responds with a smile and a gesture with her hand — "Oh, no problem. You're fine."

A few things happen right at that moment:

- The receptionist just told the client that you don't care about patients arriving on time.

- She also told the client that he can run your schedule for you, paying no mind to your needs as a professional and the needs of all your other patients.

- If your receptionist is actually doing her job correctly, she doesn't think it is "okay" for the patient to be late. Instead of addressing the issue now, she'll later gossip with the other members of your office and talk about "that patient" who is always late.

Can you see how a simple thing like telling a patient that a behavior is okay when it isn't creates a culture you don't want?

You are in charge of creating the culture you want.

In this section, I will talk about different company cultures that have stood out recently because of the way they do business. Your job is not to copy them, but to be inspired by them.

Here comes the problem. With all my research, I was hard-pressed to find a specific formula for creating a culture. There were some good ideas as to what different cultures could look like, but when it came to outlining a formula for getting the cultural outcome you desire, I couldn't find one.

I decided to break it down myself. In order to do so, I had to go back further than the 1960s and look at a time where the entire culture of our world changed. In doing so, I was able to break down exactly how you can change the culture in your business.

———

In the 1930s, two men radically changed the world. Out of a single, simple thought in their heads, they created a worldview that still affects the world to this day.

I know this might be shocking for some people to hear, but I believe Walt Disney and Adolf Hitler had similar mindsets when it came to creating the outcome they wanted. They achieved the goals they wanted in life because they understood one very important thing: how to create a culture. For the most part, creating the desired culture for both Adolf and Walt only took three simple steps:

1. Vision
2. Expectation
3. Support

When Disney came up with the idea for Disneyland, he created a very specific image that he wanted people to buy into. He had to be so clear on his vision that the investors and the creative team he surrounded himself with could fully accept and embrace the idea, as if it was their own. Once they caught hold of the vision in this manner they understood the expectations required to achieve it and knew they had the necessary support to create it.

Adolf Hitler also had a vision; an evil, terrible, awful vision, but a vision all the same. People bought into that vision because he had specific expectations that the people understood, and he gave them the support they needed as long as they were following those expectations.

However you feel about Disney or the Nazis, the point is that they understood how to create a culture that changed the world. The cultures became so strong that people, who in normal circumstances would never act in certain ways, ultimately gave up their known patterns of thought, personalities, and even civil morals in order to go along with the culture. (Although there are plenty of stories that could be told, let's not focus on the awful things would-be decent people ended up doing for the Nazi party, and focus on Disney instead.)

When you go to Disneyland, Disneyworld or any of the Disney theme parks with your family, something very interesting happens. People act differently than they do in normal life. People are willing to change otherwise everyday behavior based on the fact they are at Disneyland. You don't notice people smoking very often at the theme park. People don't sit around getting drunk. For the most part, people aren't belligerent. Yeah, on sweaty and miserable days you might have more cranky people, but in general, the moment you step through those gates you buy into the culture by accepting the vision of a magical kingdom. You go along with the expectation, and most importantly, you know that acting like a kid and having a great time will not just be supported by everyone around you, it will be encouraged.

Disney is a success because people created a culture. They know who they are and they expect everyone to agree. Not just the visitors, but everyone involved with the brand. From cast members to the creative department, called Imagineers, everyone accepts the culture of Disney.

So, how can your business be like Disney and create a culture that everyone buys into? A culture where not only the team you hire understands and helps to grow it, but all of your clients as well.

It's actually not that difficult. You simply have to put some time into being very clear on each one of these three steps: **Vision, Expectation and Support.**

Let's break down each one of these vital areas so you can start to create your own culture. I have to remind you, this is not meant to be information to read, then forget in a few months after the next consultant comes along with another idea. In order to create the success you want, there are exercises to complete at the end of each chapter. To get results, you actually have to do them.

There are enough good ideas out there. I want to emphasize that the goal is for you to *create* throughout this book, not just gain knowledge.

When you do create a culture that is uniquely yours, you will gain two very important things that your competitors do not have:

- A thriving business that your patients will want to support with referrals and amazing testimonials.

- A team of support in the office, or your practice, that cares more about the growth of the business than they do about infighting, gossip and their own selfish needs.

So, let's get started!

VISION

● ●

"A leader has the vision and conviction that a dream can be achieved. He inspires the power and energy to get it done."

— Ralph Lauren

Vision \'vi-zhen\ : the ability to see : something that you imagine : a picture you see in your mind

"A computer in every home."

"The happiest place on Earth."

"Helping others live their best life."

"Think different."

Bill Gates, Walt Disney, Oprah Winfrey, and Steve Jobs all had a vision. Because of their visions, we all live our lives differently than we did before that vision was put into motion. These visions were and are their guiding beacons.

Once they created what they envisioned, they enrolled others into that vision, and together achieved (and continue to achieve) things beyond imagination, that have literally changed the world.

Because of someone's vision, you have one, if not multiple, computers in your home and office. Because of someone's vision, you can go to a place where your imagination can run wild and your childhood dreams can come true. Because of someone's vision, you can have your phone, music, email and games all in the palm of your hand.

Richard Branson said, "If you don't dream it, nothing happens."

Is your company going to impact the world the way the iPhone or personal computer has? Will you create a brand so big that your endorsement can make a book a bestseller? Probably not.

However, that doesn't mean your vision isn't just as important as the visions of Steve Jobs or Oprah, or that it doesn't hold the same importance to your clients and your team's lives.

When you have a specific vision for your practice, you will easily create a work environment that motivates your team, energizes you, and creates raving fans of your clients.

"If you are working on something exciting that you really care about, you don't have to be pushed. The vision pulls you." – Steve Jobs

Vision is a vital aspect of effective leadership in any organization. Your practice needs a vision not just to plan where you are going, but to continuously monitor progress and stay on track.

What does a vision actually give a company?

Purpose: Compelling visions convey a larger sense of company purpose. They aren't just written statements. They have an emotional connection that resonates with your team and becomes part of the culture. Effective visions have the power to inspire and focus the efforts of your practice for years to come. Your vision is based upon the beliefs, principles and values you hold dear, and define the way you want your team to live their work lives. Your vision has to go beyond a temporary motivation or inspiration.

Clarity: Clarity is power. The confused mind says, "no" so the more clarity your vision has, the more people will say "yes" to you. It is important that everyone understands the values and purpose of the vision in order to make it real. Clear-cut visions enable employees to picture themselves helping build the company versus simply maintaining the status quo. When properly implemented, visions can be response systems that enable an organization to respond to its challenges and help leaders and teams navigate those challenges together.

Goals: In order to achieve your vision you must create achievable goals and pursue those goals relentlessly as a team. You will not achieve your goals unless your team is equally invested in the vision.

Do you have a specific vision for your practice? For your clients? Do you have a goal for your company beyond the generic, "We give great customer service", "We are well known in the community", or "We are better than our competitors"?

What is it that you really want most for your clients or patients to experience through your service?

For your practice to truly make an impact, and know what that impact actually looks like, creating a vision is a must. There are two visions you have to define in your business. First, the vision of whom your ideal client is, and second, the vision of what your company will accomplish. The easy answer is typically not the correct one in this situation.

Vision of your Client

Do you know who your ideal client is? It's the most fundamental question every business owner must answer. If your answer to that question is something along the lines of, "anyone who needs my service" then you do not know who your ideal client is. You're most likely wasting your marketing dollars.

In order to be laser-focused in your marketing efforts and get the best return on your investment, it is critical to know who you're "talking" to. You must be crystal clear on whom you want to serve. This will not only help you make the best marketing and advertising decisions, it will also help you know what you are as a company when it comes to which services you want to focus on.

For example, a *dentist* spending money to sponsor the T-ball league hoping to convert those kids — or better yet, those kids' parents — into clients makes sense because they can be clients right now. However, doing the same thing as an *orthodontist*, when those 8-10-year-olds aren't ideal clients for another at least two to four years is not the best use of your marketing dollars. Sponsoring 12-14-year-old players is more beneficial.

I know many people who spend thousands of dollars per month marketing to the wrong crowd because they do not know who their ideal client is. Or even worse, they are just giving some ad salesman disguised as a "marketer" money every month to advertise their business to the general population in generic channels like the Yellow Pages, online directories and Valu-Pak coupons... such a waste of time and money.

Creating a customer avatar is the most effective way to decide who your ideal client is. (No, I am not talking about the big blue aliens from the movie!) An avatar is an imaginary person that, when outlined correctly, will help you design a specific and more profitable marketing plan. An avatar is an incredibly effective way to get into the head of your perfect client.

A word of warning, however: Determining your avatar is not a random, piecemeal business exercise, like the way many companies treat a mission statement or core values. This is a serious and vital exercise for your practice's success.

Once you have your specific avatar defined, it will give you a point of reference to determine the answers to the following questions:

- **Where should you advertise** in order to achieve maximum exposure to reach your client?

- **What types of advertising** and marketing materials affect your ideal client the most?

- **What images, language and tone** should you use in your marketing materials, website and public image?

- **What story should your content be telling** that they could relate to?

Another powerful advantage that comes from knowing your avatar is in your expert positioning (which we will cover in the Relationship section). Your avatar will set you apart from your competition. You can become the specialist for your desired type of client.

1. What is the client's name, age, ethnicity, education?

   _____

   _____

   _____

2. What is the client's average yearly income?

   _____

3. What are the client's buying habits?

   _____

   _____

   _____

4. What is important to the client?

_____

_____

_____

_____

5. What is the client's biggest problem / challenge?

_____

_____

_____

_____

6. What are the client's values, attitudes, and needs?

_____

_____

_____

_____

If this sounds more involved than you thought, good! It is. And it is really important if you want to gain the best return on your investment in all your marketing and advertising. Below is an example of a fully developed avatar for an orthodontist who wants to be the doctor all the local high school kids go to.

Jamie is a 16-year-old local high school student. She is active, outgoing and the oldest of three siblings. She loves social media but is focused on her education as well. Her parents couldn't afford braces when she was younger but now dad has new insurance that covers enough of the investment for it to be financially feasible. However, Jamie is two years away from graduating and doesn't want to be in braces during her last two years of high school. She shudders to think that her yearbook pictures and her graduation photo will show a bunch of metal in her mouth.

Now, with Jamie as your avatar, where would you focus your marketing and advertising efforts if you were an orthodontist?

Write down some ideas:

_____

_____

_____

_____

_____

_____

_____

_____

(Seriously, pull out a pen and write down some ideas above before reading on! You don't have to be right; you just have to be willing to experiment with ideas.)

Here are a few that would make sense:

- Market the benefits of Invisalign® (a removable, clear teeth-straightening tray system) to students.

- Post pictures and advertisements on Instagram. (Teenagers are not on Facebook that much any more, by the way.) You have to know and go where your market is. Use the hashtag (#) of your local high school, and show teenagers with Invisalign® or invisible braces. (This hashtag idea is a 5 figure-plus idea if you use it correctly.)

- As summer approaches, use advertising headlines like "Straighten your teeth this summer without having to get braces", "Want that perfect graduation smile without needing braces?" or "Teenage teeth-straightening specialists."

With the right marketing, there is truly no short supply of possible clients. (If you're an orthodontist, there will always be teenagers who need their teeth straightened.)

No matter what your profession, once word gets out about what you've done for people, the referrals will keep things rolling.

Because the doctor in my example wants to serve the high school market, his avatar is going to be a bit different than if he were focusing on the 12 to 14-year-old market. Why? Because high school students tend to have more of an opinion when it comes to their looks than 12 or 13-year-olds.

If he were to focus on the 12 to 14-year-old market, his avatar would need to be created based on the decision-maker, typically the parent.

The avatar on the previous page is for the patient. What happens when the patient and the client are not the same? As in my example of Jamie, she is the patient you are marketing your service to, but her parents are the clients who will ultimately make the buying decision.

Do you have to have an avatar for both the patient and the client? In this case, I believe you would be well served to do so.

Does it change up your advertising and marketing? It does, but only a little. If you are going to advertise in the school's yearbook, newsletter or lunchroom, then your message should be focused on the patient avatar. However, if you are advertising in your local newspaper, movie theater or even on the banners at the baseball field, then focusing on the parent avatar would suit you best.

The point is to create focused (or rifled) marketing, based upon your ideal client and patient versus shotgun-based marketing to everyone.

When you start thinking of your avatar as a living, breathing person whose problems or needs you can solve, suddenly your marketing dollars are much more effective.

Are you ready to create your avatar?

Go to thepracticecure.com and sign up for *The Path to the Propreneur*. You'll be able to access the Avatar training with printable PDF forms to help you.

Company Vision

Now it's time to focus on your practice.

What is it you want most for your clients or patients to experience through your service?

What is the reason you got into your business in the first place?

Honestly, for some professionals, it is purely a financial play. For the most part, there is nothing wrong with that. However, I believe that if you are reading a book like this, you have a deeper reason for choosing your profession.

Maybe it's because you received amazing care from a doctor after an accident when you were a kid and it stuck with you. Maybe you had funky teeth growing up like me and never smiled in school pictures until a caring orthodontist gave you a smile that you love to show off. Or perhaps you had a car accident and were told you would never walk again until a passionate chiropractor gave you back your mobility.

That is where your vision started, fueling the drive to do what you do. Have you forgotten that? Have you lost your focus, or do you feel like it was taken from you with all the business needs, employee drama and client complaints?

It's time to get back to that, but now, let's go bigger.

One of my chiropractor client's visions is to be the first thought in his patients' minds when it comes to their health care.

One orthodontist student has the goal "to be the best part of my patients' day," while another has the focus to "design a reason for you to smile the rest of your life."

If you could wave your magic wand and make sure that every single client, patient or customer received 'X', what would that be? When I ask this question, I'm not asking it rhetorically. I really want you to sit down and think: "What is the experience I want my patients or clients to have before, during and after they come to my business?"

When was the last time you felt you got amazing customer service? What was the difference? If you backtrack through the entire experience, I would bet that you'll see your feeling comes from not just one big moment, but a collection of value-added moments before, during and after your experience, all of them in alignment with that company's big vision.

If you want your clients to have a consistent and memorable experience that will help them know what your vision is for them, and if you want to separate yourself from every other business like

> Your vision is not just a simple motivator. It should pervade everything you do.

yours, then your vision must show up in everything. From your initial marketing to your follow-up after the transaction, your vision must permeate how you treat your clients throughout the process.

Your vision is not just a simple motivator. It should pervade everything you do. It attracts the best clients. It gives you energy everyday as you walk into the office and gives you a sense of accomplishment when you walk out at night. It helps you decide whether you're going to take one path or another. Your vision is your compass.

When you make vision-based decisions, you don't just feel good about them. The vision becomes your "source" or your anchor. You won't typically doubt or second-guess yourself. The hiring and firing decisions, educational choices and the consultants you choose to bring in will all be in alignment with the vision you've created.

That is, if you have a strong one.

Without a strong vision, you flounder and end up not quite knowing exactly what you want. Your business never seems to align with you. As a matter of fact, without a vision, the people in your life — your clients, family members, friends, and especially your office team — will not understand what your ideal looks like, and, more importantly, how they can help you create it. You are doing a major disservice to your company and everyone involved, including yourself, if you don't have a strong vision to guide it.

If you are an orthodontist, you obviously want your patients to have straight teeth. But is that all? Do you just want them to have straight teeth, or do you want them to have such a great experience with your practice that they are referring everybody to you? Wouldn't you want them to brag about you? Wouldn't you want them to advocate for you so passionately that they feel anyone who is not coming to you is crazy?

You don't want people coming to you based upon price, location or a local ad they saw. You want people to come to you based on the experience you provide. When you have a vision, you can create something much more powerful for you *and* for your clients.

Your vision is your anchor not only during the ups, but also when your business isn't going as well as you'd like. I used to have a mentor who said, *"Murphy visits all of us."*

Without the anchor of a vision, when "Murphy" visits your office or your life, it takes three to four times longer to bounce back. With a vision, recovery can happen within days, and in some cases, hours.

Have I beaten this drum loudly enough? This is an area that has been proven over and over again to fail professional practices. The lack of one is the exact reason the culture in your practice is weak or nonexistent. You cannot build an awesome culture without a specific, strong vision.

I used to have a mentor who said, *"Murphy visits all of us."*

At this point, I hope you are wondering how to develop a vision like this, or that you're considering the need to revisit the vision you thought you had.

If you think you have a clear vision that permeates to your desired client, let's put it to the test.

First, look at your marketing and advertising efforts. Beyond the colors and the images used, is it all really any different than your competitors'? Does it actually *say something* about you and your vision, and the value you are trying to give?

If you are a dentist, is the only thing that separates your message from your competitors' message the "free" toothbrush, teeth whitening or exam that you are offering?

For the orthodontist, are you touting your different style of "bands" as your value add, knowing that your potential patients have no idea what the difference is?

Are you an attorney who offers a "we don't get paid unless you do" incentive?

These are not vision-driven ads. These are just rinsed and repeated filler.

The reason why so many professional practices don't focus as much as they should on their vision is because of the work involved. However, the practices that make the effort, change it up and create a specific vision are the memorable ones that clients everywhere freely talk about (a.k.a. *promote*).

That is why you are here.

Your first assignment is to create and write down your vision.

EXERCISE: *Creating Your Vision*

In order to be successful in defining your vision, there are two parts that need to be formed. First is the ultimate goal, or "new world order," that you want to create. Second is what feeds the vision in order for that to happen — your core values.

The core values are the habits you and your team create. It will help you take your huge vision and make it something that you can start implementing today. We will cover how to create those in the next section, Expectations.

It's important to scale down this exercise into bite-size chunks in order to create both.

I'd like to walk you through a few steps on how to do that, and please make sure you actually do this as an exercise. Write it down as I walk you through it. Do not put it off until the end of the book.

In order to get you into the right mindset, I have two rules that will serve you well when followed:

Rule #1: When you answer the questions, don't edit yourself. Whatever your primal brain says, write it down. This is not a time to worry about what is "normal" in your field or to listen to the little voices in your head about what can/cannot be done. Your colleagues or peers do not get a vote in this decision. Your vision is yours and yours alone. Do not hold back.

Rule #2: You might find that your vision cannot actually be completely accomplished in this lifetime. Accept that fact. For example, in my marriage-mentoring program, The Business of Marriage, my goal is to reverse the direction of divorce in the country, and then the world. My logical brain knows that it's a huge goal, and probably not attainable in my lifetime. However, it's the thing that incessantly drives me when I'm having a bad day. It's okay to have a vision that is bigger than you are.

1. What is it that I want? What do I see?

   _____

   _____

   _____

   _____

   _____

   _____

   _____

2. Why do I want it?

_____

_____

_____

_____

3. What would it do for me:

   a. Personally?

_____

_____

_____

_____

   b. Professionally?

_____

_____

_____

_____

   c. Emotionally?

_____

_____

_____

_____

   d. Physically?

_____

_____

_____

_____

4. What are some of the positive qualities your clients have shared about your practice?

_____

_____

_____

_____

_____

_____

_____

5. What is the most important quality you think your practice has?

_____

_____

_____

_____

_____

_____

_____

6. Imagine yourself in 20 years. What impression would you like to leave on your:

   a. Profession?

_____

_____

_____

_____

_____

_____

_____

b. Your community?

_____

_____

_____

_____

_____

_____

_____

7. What is unique about your practice? (2nd generation, same location for a long time, specialize in certain cases)

_____

_____

_____

_____

_____

_____

8. Who in your profession (or others) has a practice you admire?

_____

_____

_____

_____

_____

_____

9. If you could create a similar practice, what would it say to your peers?

_____

_____

_____

_____

_____

_____

_____

10. What needs to change to realize it?

_____

_____

_____

_____

_____

_____

_____

_____

_____

11. What will this say about you?

_____

_____

_____

_____

_____

_____

12. How will this affect your team?

_____

_____

_____

_____

_____

_____

_____

13. How will this affect your family?

_____

_____

_____

_____

_____

_____

_____

_____

_____

14. How will this affect your clients?

_____

_____

_____

_____

_____

_____

15. How will this vision help your industry?

_____

_____

_____

_____

_____

_____

_____

16. What will you need from your team in order to make it happen?

_____

_____

_____

_____

_____

_____

_____

_____

17. What is your vision? (Don't edit, just write.)

_____

_____

_____

_____

_____

_____

18. Go through your answers and find power words or phrases that resonate with you (i.e. heartfelt, generational, design, create, hope).

_____

_____

_____

_____

_____

_____

_____

19. Write a statement that combines your vision and the words you chose.

_____

_____

_____

_____

_____

_____

_____

20. Edit it down to a more concise statement.

_____

_____

_____

_____

_____

_____

_____

Does your vision fit your needs? Does it motivate? Does it combine all that you want for your clients?

Now that you have a true vision, you will want to decide on a few things that promote that vision in a manner that makes sense. (In other words, consider how you are going to integrate this vision into your branding, marketing and advertising.)

Need more guidance with your vision?

Go to **thepracticecure.com** to gain access to the in-depth vision training, as well as a PDF download of the questions above.

Chapter Takeaway:

- The most fundamental question every business owner must answer is, *"Do you know who your ideal client is?"*

- Your customer avatar is a guiding point for critical decisions in your business — decisions that involve *all* of your marketing efforts.

- In order for your vision to play out, it must be specific and strong. It is not simply a motivator. It should pervade everything you do.

- Your vision acts as an anchor for all decisions in your business.

EXPECTATIONS

"Don't lower your expectations to meet your performance. Raise your level of performance to meet your expectations. Expect the best of yourself, and then do what is necessary to make it a reality."

— *Ralph Marston*

Before I go out to an office for training, I send a survey to the entire team. Among other things, the survey asks the employees if they feel as though they fully understand all the expectations required to perform their jobs, and if they feel they are given all the necessary tools and support they need.

I also send a separate survey to the owner in order to find out if he or she believes everyone understands his or her expectations.

It's very interesting to see how many of the employees are not entirely sure of what is expected, compared to the owner's confidence that they have a fully informed team. Some employees will even comment specifically about their "shifting" duties and the "lack of support" they feel when it comes to doing their jobs.

I don't want it to sound like these offices have no direction and are run without any structure. The surveys only tell me that there is always room for improvement in clarity of communication, especially when it comes to expectations. Clarity always brings power and confidence.

The survey discloses the false assumption that everybody on the team fully understands the expectation of the owner. This lack of clarity is often the cause of disagreements, backbiting, hurt feelings and other disruptions in the flow of the practice.

If one person is not living up to the expectations either out of choice or ignorance, it brings the energy of the entire office down. This will bring conflict in your office because one person will assume an expectation of something, while the other person does not. Therefore, neither parties' expectations are going to be met, feelings will be hurt, and the energy level will drop.

If everyone understands the expectations because you have laid them out as the owner of the business, then it makes it a lot easier for people to choose to either rise to those expectations or elect to work somewhere else.

When everyone knows their specific expectations, they will not only get along better, they will perform better for you and your clients.

As a bonus, clear expectations allow people to choose whether they want to go above and beyond, or hit below expectations. They will be happy to go the extra mile when they are asked because they don't feel underappreciated for the work they are doing.

There are four types of expectations in a practice:

1. **Specific Individual Expectations:** What each person must do to perform their individual job to their best ability (take X-rays, fill out the chart correctly, assist the doctor, etc.).

2. **General Team Expectations:** The basic duties as a member of the team (being on time, dressing in a professional manner, using professional language, etc.).

3. **Company Core Values:** The requirements for everyone in the office in order for your vision to play out.

4. **Client Expectations:** What is expected of your clients and how you enforce that (show up on time, take care of the things you ask them to, etc.).

For the purposes of this book, we are going to focus on how to create the first three points. What you expect from each client will vary based upon your industry. However, once you start to implement these first three elements, you will be surprised how infectious they will be to your clients. They will naturally start treating you and their responsibility as a client different based upon the expectations you have created within your practice.

Specific Individual Expectations

Individual Expectations depend on a person's job title and position. Do not assume that your team understands this! Make sure you are reviewing each team members' expectations on a consistent basis, individually. Have them write up exactly what they think it is, then review it and make the appropriate corrections. Some might need more training in a particular area, when you just assumed they knew what to do.

Recently, I had a finance manager of an orthodontic office contact me. She was frustrated with a team member (we will call her Sue) who had been working in the office for eight years. The manager's complaint was that Sue continually marked the wrong insurance information on the chart. This was a major mistake that not only caused the finance manager to have to do more work than necessary, but, in some cases, was illegal.

The manager was at a loss as to why Sue, who had been there for so long, kept making the mistake. Even though the manager had pointed out the mistake multiple times, it was as if Sue just couldn't understand that it was creating a negative environment for the manager. (I know some of you are thinking, "Why doesn't the manager just go to the owner for some disciplinary action if it keeps persisting?" We will get to the reason why in the Responsibility section.)

I gave the manager a few ideas on how to approach Sue in a new way. One was to find out Sue's learning style. Sue might be told audibly what to do, but if her learning style is visual or tactile, then the message will not be fully received. Once the manager understood Sue's learning style, she could retrain her on what was expected.

Many managers and owners hold a false belief that if they get more and more exasperated when they point out a mistake, the offender will eventually understand and change the behavior. This clearly is not so. If the employee either does not understand why it's needed or doesn't believe it is actually an expectation for the specific job, expressing frustration will not create a new behavior. A manager needs to enroll an employee into a new expectation by showing her the requirement using the style of learning that will have the greatest impact. (I will go more into how learning styles can transform the way your team responds to you in the Excellence chapter.)

General Team Expectations

General Team Expectations are another element that comes across as straightforward — but that is often not the case. Of course, there will be the occasional exception to the rule, but for the practice as a whole, the *expectations should be the same* for every member of the team. If not, you can definitely expect internal backbiting and frustration within the office.

This includes you as the leader of the team. You must live by the expectations you set for the team. Do not be fooled into the idea that because you are the boss, there are different rules that apply you. "Do what I say, not what I do" does not work if you want to be a great leader and have a team that respects you.

To give a positive example, during every holiday season at Zappos, every employee in every department is expected to spend 10 hours on the customer service line to help with the high demand. CEO Tony Hsieh still clocks in his 10 hours every year. (This is also a great example of the need for cross training within your team.)

It's important for you to hold your team to those expectations. If you have one team member who is habitually late, or often takes off time from work, or leaves early because little Johnny needs this or that without you knowing ahead of time, thus breaking the expectation that everybody stays until 5 o 'clock, then that one person is going to bring down the energy of everyone in the office.

It's a ripple effect. No matter how much everyone will tell you "Oh it's fine. We understand," they don't, and they won't, and it will be a challenge in your office.

"Janet" was a treatment coordinator, or TC, in a Northern California office. She had been with the practice for over 10 years. She developed a habit that even the doctor at first brushed off, but it became an annoyance he never addressed. Every time the office would take some time off for vacation or what have you, Janet would take an extra day, either before or after everyone else. Janet's husband worked for an airline so she could get stand-by tickets, and it was best to go the day before a holiday or come home the day after. It made sense.

At first, no one seemed to mind. However, it became so common that it was eventually expected. The day before a vacation or the day after, the TC, the one person in the office in charge of closing the sale, signing contracts and starting the treatment process, was not in the office. The team got used to not having any new starts for those days. Do you think it did not affect them in a negative way? When it came to hitting monthly goals, and they missed by just a few starts or collected dollars, do you think some were thinking about the lost days?

When you don't have clear and concise General Team Expectations, the loss of morale, team togetherness, and trust in general, is the obvious result.

Decide what General Team Expectations you want according to your vision of the way you want your office to run. What are the expectations you want everyone to meet every day? What are the high-level expectations to make sure your office is running at its optimal performance? It's something very easy to do; yet, when expectations are not met, it causes a lot of disruption inside the office.

Outline the expectations, write them down, and make sure everybody knows them. Following that, hold a team meeting and talk about your vision and expectations, and allow your team to be engaged in that conversation. You might have to enroll some or all of your team members into your expectation all over again.

A powerful way to enroll them is to have them work with you to create them. People support what they create, so make your life easier by truly making it a team effort. You will be surprised what they come up with.

Once the expectations are set, if someone doesn't meet them, it's easier for you to be able to point out the incongruence — and as the leader, take the necessary action.

Company Core Values

A moment ago I mentioned Zappos. They are known for their extraordinary customer service. That service is created with a very strong and specific set of core values.

What if you had a practice where the core values were so, well... valued, that your team would rather take a $2,000 payout to quit their jobs before they would choose not to uphold them? That is what happens at Zappos.

Tony Hsieh is so passionate about making sure every person supports the company's core values (including himself), that after a new hire goes through the training process, he offers anyone who is not willing to be in alignment with those values a no-questions, guilt or shame payout of $2,000 to quit and go work somewhere else.

Unfortunately, most companies create core values (if they create any at all) as part of a generic business check-off-list that doesn't really guide them. Saying "We give great customer service", "We value our customers" or "We get the job done right the first time" has nothing to do with the vision and the real culture you want to create. (Besides, what company doesn't claim all of those?)

I would even guess that most owners don't even know what true core values are.

A very simple way to test whether your core values are generic is to give them the "I would hope so" test. If after reviewing a potential value, your knee-jerk response would be to say, "I would hope so", then that value has failed. (Didn't you say that to yourself when you read those examples above?)

"We give great customer service..." *I would hope so!*

"We value our customers…" *I would hope so!*

"We get the job done right, the first time…" *I would hope so!*

These are examples of what meaningful core values are NOT!

Core values are specific values that impact a company's culture, brand and strategies. They are NOT generic, meaningless words. Unique core values set you apart from other companies and help drive success.

I often refer to them as the Hiring and Firing List. Your core values should be so tuned in to what you are as a company and what you expect in order to obtain your vision that you could use them as the primary qualifications in searching for new employees, as well as the guidelines for your employee reviews.

Your core values are the direct roadmap for reaching your company vision.

It can also be used as a powerful "how we do business" guideline. It cuts through the "but I like them as a person" or "but they have kids" or "but they have been here for so long" excuses so many owners use when it comes to hanging onto employees that should have been invited to work somewhere else a long time ago.

On a recent coaching call with Dr. Joe and his wife Jan, Jan expressed frustration that the office management was having with her husband. Dr. Joe had built a great management team for his five dentistry practices. He had recently stepped more into the role of manager, having to do less of the actual practice work. His son, the CEO, had learned the ropes from his father and was doing a great job in his role.

Dr. Joe and Jan had gone away on a two-week cruise, leaving the practice in the hands of his CEO and the other management team members. Upon Dr. Joe's return, his management team informed him of some serious infractions committed by one of the associates while he was away, and the team had decided he needed to be fired. They were just in need of his final approval.

Dr. Joe wasn't sure. In general, this associate seemed to be a good guy, and going through the hassle of finding/training another associate was not something he was looking forward to. After hearing the complaints and the associate's excuses, he ultimately decided to go against the management team and not fire the associate.

This caused obvious strain within the management team, leaving them to wonder why they were left in charge if they weren't allowed to do their jobs. It only took a few more months of the associate, with his newfound boldness, to cause additional problems for the team before Dr. Joe was forced to comply with previous requests and fire him.

Now he was not only down an associate, he was dealing with a management team that felt like they could not be trusted.

When I received the call, Dr. Joe and Jan were about to embark on another vacation. Jan's concern was obvious. How could Dr. Joe stop that from happening again, and keep ultimate control of his practice?

The simple answer I gave was the root of the original problem. The company needed to have its core values set in place and agreed upon by all involved. It was imperative to create specific core values that would help guide the team in any and every decision.

Had they put the core values in place and had they actually taken them seriously, his management team would have been able to use the guidelines for their initial discussion. Dr. Joe would have been able to make his decision based upon the core values they all shared.

Having a specific set of strong, vision-centered core values in place creates a sense of security and trust for a management team, provides deeper expectations for employees and gives an owner the ability to lead according to his vision.

So how do you create a great set of core values? Below is an exercise you can use to flush out what you really want to apply as your core values. You can do this exercise alone, but I suggest you involve your entire team. As I mentioned earlier, people support what they create. So the instructions are given as if you are walking your team through the exercise.

Want more help creating core values?

This process can seem daunting. Follow along with a training video and print off a PDF download for your team to fill out at thepracticecure.com.

EXERCISE: Core Values

First let's look at some examples of vision-centered core values from other companies.

Zappos: We deliver WOW customer service! Embrace and drive change. Do more with less. Build a positive team and family spirit.

TOMS Shoes: Give sustainably and responsibly. Help have a bigger impact on the world. Welcome feedback to help us improve.

Google: Do one thing really, really well. You don't need to be at your desk to need an answer. You can make money without doing evil. You can be serious without a suit.

Datwyler Orthodontics: Every patient a Rock Star, Radiate professionalism, Have only good days and great days, Provide solutions, Advocate for the practice.

Our Ripple Effect, Inc. (me): Create random acts of WOW-ness, Take chances, Be inquisitive, Honor the journey, Act from your highest self, Bring the joy.

As you can see, successful companies have specific core values that directly align with their image and vision. In many of these you can actually see part of their vision in their values.

Okay. Let's get started.

In order to know what you want for your practice, you first need to know what *you* value. List five core values you want for yourself, personally.

1. _____
2. _____
3. _____
4. _____
5. _____

List five core values you want for your company.

1. _____
2. _____
3. _____
4. _____
5. _____

Next, partner up with one other team member! Share your personal core values and company core values. Which values are similar?

1. _____
2. _____
3. _____
4. _____
5. _____

Share your core values with everyone. List similarities on a master list.

_____

_____

_____

_____

_____

Now, look at all the values you've listed. These values are good. They're all very nice and comfortable, but we aren't here to be nice and comfortable! We are here to push you to the next level, outside of your comfort zone.

In my live trainings, I tell the teams that at this point, if they do not doubt their ability to uphold these values, then we are not hitting hard enough. (Not that I want anyone to quit, but if they aren't a bit uncomfortable, maybe even considering Zappos' $2,000 payout, thinking, "Wow! This is pushing a few of my comfort buttons," then we need to dig deeper.)

You are not going for good core values; you are going for the best.

You don't want a company that is basic or standard. You want a company that gives *exceptional* service.

There is a difference between a value that says, "We have good attitudes" and a company that says, "We only have good days and great days."

When you find core values that push you outside of your comfort circle, something phenomenal happens. You've taken professionalism a step further — there's passion behind it! You're excited to show up to work because you have goals you're reaching as a team. You're engaged with the clients because you care about their satisfaction, not just your pay. You've gone beyond being an employee. You are a team member that is contributing to the bigger picture and the core values of the company.

Break into groups of three. Take 10 minutes and brainstorm the words for core values that will take the original words you wrote down to the next level.

_____

_____

_____

_____

_____

_____

_____

_____

_____

_____

Next, take 5 minutes to find or create at least 5 core values you are all passionate about.

1. _____

2. _____

3. _____

4. _____
5. _____
6. _____
7. _____
8. _____
9. _____
10. _____

Now, have each group present their 5 core values to the entire group, and then explain why you are passionate about them. (Passion wins, so be passionate!)

Create a master list of the top core values.

_____
2. _____
3. _____
4. _____
5. _____
6. _____
7. _____
8. _____
9. _____
10. _____
11. _____
12. _____
13. _____
14. _____
15. _____
16. _____
17. _____

18. _____
19. _____
20. _____
21. _____
22. _____
23. _____
24. _____
25. _____

Time to finalize! As a group, decide on the words that support your vision. Ideally, you'll have no more than 15 values that represent the desires of the entire office.

1. _____
2. _____
3. _____
4. _____
5. _____
6. _____
7. _____
8. _____
9. _____
10. _____
11. _____
12. _____
13. _____
14. _____
15. _____

Chapter Takeaway:

- When the four types of expectations (**Specific individual, General Team, Core Values and Client**) are clearly defined, people rise to the occasion and achieve greater success.

- Your core values are your direct roadmap for reaching your vision.

- Your core values and your vision are the mold that shapes your company's culture.

- People support what they create. When creating your core values, enroll your team to create them with you.

SUPPORT

"Employee loyalty begins with employer loyalty. Your employees should know that if they do the job they were hired to do with a reasonable amount of competence and efficiency, you will support them."

— Harvey Mackay

Now that you have a clear vision and have created specific expectations for your team, the last necessary element in creating your culture is helping them know they are supported.

This is the fastest way to develop the best performance from each team member. When they know you support them, they will feel you trust them, leading to respect. In the book *Crucial Conversations* by Kerry Patterson says, "respect is like air. You don't really notice it until it's not there... then it's all you can think about." Respect is crucial for team unity.

Does your team know that they are supported in making general decisions without your specific say so, or do they live in fear of making a mistake, not wanting to take ownership of their position?

Let's use the Disney example again. Imagine for a second that you are a Disney World Adventureland street sweeper. You spend all day, every day cleaning up after people to make sure your section of the Magic Kingdom looks pristine and brilliant for every guest. You understand that in order for every guest to feel like it is the

"Happiest Place on Earth," your job expectation is to quickly and efficiently pick up every piece of trash, sweep up every kernel of popcorn and mop up every spilled ice cream cone in Adventureland. You happily take care of your section of the park and take pride in doing your job.

One day as you are cleaning up, a guest comes up to you, pushing three small kids in a stroller, and asks how they can get to Dumbo's Daring Adventure in Fantasyland... two "lands" away.

You stop what you are doing and escort her to the closest entrance to Fantasyland and Dumbo's ride is in her view.

Even though this act takes you out of your assigned area and away from your immediate duties, you know your supervisor and everyone up the chain of command will support your decision.

Why?

Because you are acting in the best interest of the vision of the company and you are in alignment with the *expectations* of your job.

Your team clearly understands your vision for the company and the expectations you have for them. Now, all they need to know is that they have your full support to execute their jobs correctly. In doing so, the "It's not my job" attitude will not rear its ugly head in your business.

Support Brings Empowerment

When you *truly* support your team, you are empowering them. When they feel empowered, they believe in their own ability to make decisions and take action.

Some employers that say they want to empower their employees rarely truly mean it. (It's like you as a parent saying to a teenage child that you want him to tell you the "truth". In reality, unless the truth is that he didn't go out and party on Friday night and chose to do volunteer work at an elderly home instead, you don't really want to hear it.)

Likewise, the employer wants the employee to feel "empowered" as long as that means the employee will do things the way the employer would do it. It's a nice buzzword that gives the illusion of leadership, but it is not actually serving anyone. It will often cause further distrust in employees.

> Some employers that say they want to empower their employees rarely *truly* mean it.

Even the employers who truly want to empower their teams usually do not know how to approach it. They use the word "empowerment" as a way to delegate responsibility and hope the employee knows what they are doing. We will cover delegation in an upcoming chapter, but for now, let's look at what it takes to *actually* empower your employees.

In a 2011 blog post, Nevada Management Professor Bret Simmons suggested a winning formula for creating true workplace empowerment that includes "positive leadership (e.g. trust, authenticity, support), high-performance managerial practices (e.g. training, rewards, recognition, participatory decision making), social / political support (e.g. access to resources, information sharing, fairness), and work characteristics (interesting work with a variety of different tasks)."

How you implement that formula is part of the reason you are reading this book in the first place.

Let's look at **five key areas** in which you can show real leadership that will lead to employee empowerment.

1. **Authentically show that you value them as a member of your team.** Even though you will be better equipped to hire the best people for your needs because you have a hiring and firing list with your specific core values, it still holds true that each person is a unique individual that needs to feel valued. Through your words, your actions and your body language, people can feel if you are being genuine with them. Whether they are struggling or thriving, it is important to know that you value them as people.

2. **Continually share your vision, goals and progress with your team.** We've already talked about the importance of having a specific vision for your practice. Sharing your vision and goals needs to become a regular practice. When you do this, it brings them to the forefront of your employees' minds and will help them make decisions that are in alignment with the goals you have set.

3. **Ask better questions so you can provide guidance.** I often say that the quality of your life is based upon the quality of the questions you ask. For our purposes, you can replace the word "life" with business. All too often, owners wait for the question to be asked before they provide guidance. However, getting in the habit of taking initiative and asking great questions will help your team members feel valued, as long as it is in the tone of information-gathering and wanting to provide guidance. The better the question, the more you reduce the number of corrections that will have to be made.

   > The quality of your life is based upon the quality of the questions you ask.

4. **Continually appreciate and acknowledge your team's efforts.** Your team wants to do more for you and will do more

96

if you simply make the effort to continually recognize their efforts. Employees who feel they are undercompensated, under-noticed and underappreciated will not be willing to go the extra mile for you. They will punch their time card and do their jobs, but don't expect them to give you more time or voluntary energy if you are not willing to recognize them.

The fifth key is a bit more involved and is the most crucial if you really want your team to feel empowered. All the previous keys are something you can accomplish on your own, while the fifth key requires you to understand a bit more about them personally.

The one element of the equation that must be understood is how each person feels support. Without this, you will not get the comprehensive results you are hoping for.

5. **Recognize how each team member as an individual feels supported.** Not all people feel support in the same way, so how do you show the proper support for each team member to create a sense of empowerment? Most practices go the cash bonus route. However, studies have shown that cash is not always king when making people feel like you truly support them. In order to get the best from them, it becomes a matter of supporting them in the way they most need and feel support.

There are five ways people typically feel supported:
1. Acknowledgement
2. Things
3. Autonomy
4. Oversight
5. Education

> Don't know the questions to ask?
> *There's an assessment for that.*
>
> I have developed a specific assessment to help you learn how to best support them. You can find that assessment along with a video training at thepracticecure.com.

Through your interaction with your team, it is important to find out how they individually want to feel supported. If you don't know, ask them. However, because most people are not usually asked how they are best supported, some might not be able to give you an honest answer.

Weak owners will take the attitude of not caring, or thinking that this is too much work for them to do for an "employee." I guarantee you, if you put a little effort in this area, your team members will return it tenfold. You cannot have a dedicated and strong team if they do not feel your support.

> **WARNING!**
>
> Do not make the mistake of overlooking this vital area in creating your office culture.

Once you know your team's individual support style, here are some simple ways to show that support.

Acknowledgement: Encouraging statements. *("You're doing a great job," "Thank you for all your effort," "I couldn't have done this without you," "You are a great leader," "Good job on the _____ today.")* This can be done both in and out of earshot of others. You can make a specific time to give acknowledgements as well, like at your morning meetings.

Things: This can be anything from a simple computer-printed award to a day at the spa, gift certificates, PTO (paid time off), or more responsibility. Anything they can actually see, touch or feel that has a perceived value.

Autonomy: Allow them the ability to work on their own. Give them space, maybe a quiet place to work, to do their job, or give them the ability to telecommute, or the ability to come in on non-patient hours. Give them the direction for an assignment, a deadline and allow them to finish the assignment on their own.

Oversight: Create check-in periods. Have a process that allows them to check in with a supervisor or a manager. Create a specific daily or weekly reporting system. Make sure you or your management team is available for questions and guidance.

Education: Send them to continual education seminars, workshops or conferences. Provide educational material that is appropriate for the assignment. To really feed this style, give them opportunities to learn skills not specific to the job, but that will benefit the company.

None of these support styles are inherently better than the other. The only difference is in how your team members perceive one over another. If for whatever reason you can't give a certain team member his or her primary way of feeling supported in the moment, still show it in one of the other ways. It will be appreciated.

The importance of knowing how to support your team stems from the basic desire every work team has, and that desire is the same for you and me and every person on this planet.

Everyone has the basic desire to know three things:

1. That you **see** them.

2. That you **hear** them.

3. That what they do and say **matters** to you.

Following the five support styles will show them the support they crave and allow you to truly empower them in their positions. When you fully support your employees, you will have a team that works harder, smarter and causes less drama. More importantly, your team will become your personal marketing team that promotes, creates and celebrates you and your office.

All three main areas of vision, expectation and support create the true culture of success in your office. One cannot work without the other. If you have no vision, then how can your team members give you the real support you need, or feel like they are being supported in their work? If you have no specific expectations, then chaos eventually ensues and you breed an office with backbiting, gossip, and a lackluster work ethic. Worst of all, your office becomes just like every other office in your clients' eyes. Their decision to do business with you is based upon the location or price, not loyalty and service.

The ripple effect of creating a true and unique culture in your office will be huge. Do not be surprised if you have clients who ask about the "new feeling" or the "different atmosphere" in the office. The power of your culture will work like a magnet that attracts new clients, employees and partnerships that are in alignment with what you are creating. As you can see, creating a culture of success is not a secret; it's a system.

Chapter Takeaway:

- The quickest path to developing the best performance is to support each team member with the support style that resonates with him or her.

- You empower every person on your team by authentically showing them that they matter, enrolling them in your vision, appreciating their efforts and asking better questions.

"I am the visionary for my business and I didn't own that before. Now, I own that I am the visionary for the business. As a result, now I understand the positive side effects.

I can display the vision, but I have to have expectations. I have to set clear goals and have systems in place to achieve those visions, or else it's going to break down.

You have to take the time to master the system, work out all the kinks, write it down and then train it and reinforce it.

In the past with my staff and with my doctors, I realized that I wasn't laying down clear expectations for them. As a result, we were just going day to day rather than looking to the future. I realized that my office has to have a motivation and a vision for greater. That's what I've really owned into the last couple of years. That has allowed me to now make this leap of faith and know that it can continue. It may not continue exactly how I would want it to, but as long as they are following the system, they are allowed to put their personality into that and the practice is super successful that way.

To be successful, you have to determine your vision first and foremost. You have to define what success is.

Begin with the end in mind."

Dr. Kristina Stitcher, DC
Family First Chiropractic and Wellness

PART TWO

Operations

OPERATIONS

- -

"In the end, all business operations can be reduced to three words: people, product and profits."

— Lee Iacocca

In a small military town in Killeen, Texas, you'll find The Smile Doctors (formerly Central Texas Orthodontics). As a husband and wife team, Dr. Scott and Jessica Law have created a remarkably unique orthodontic office. It's probably one of the most, if not **the** most, successful single dental practices in the country. They have created a culture of success that is used as an example to others in the field.

It doesn't look or feel like the "typical" dental office — you know, the ones that look like they have not updated the décor in at least ten years, where the most prominent feature is a Disney movie on repeat with dim lighting, soft music, and a choice of reading materials between six-month-old entertainment magazines or a torn up children's book.

When I walked into their office for the first time, it was unlike any other dental or orthodontic office (and I have seen my fair share). The open, bright, natural-lit area is refreshing and inviting. The décor is fresh and up-to-date. The bold red and white projects a clean, modern look. It's like walking into an Apple store for your teeth.

As you walk through the open area to the reception desk, you'll be greeted by their awaiting *guest concierges* instead of "front desk girls" or "receptionists." Like when going to an upscale hotel, these people are dedicated to greeting and talking to you, not answering the phones. As a matter of fact, there are no ringing phones in this area. Another wow factor: when they see you, they actually stand to greet you.

That's just the beginning. From a massage room to a green room where you can take your picture with a silly hat and crazy background, they have created a business operation unlike anything in an orthodontic office before, and one that I hope more people will model.

While you wait, it is not uncommon to hear a song or a cheer for the latest patient who is either getting his or her braces on or off that day. The team wears matching outfits with clear name badges. They are smiling or quietly singing along to the music, walking with an eager skip in their step, and they seem to be genuinely excited to be there. The energy causes a potential new patient to think, "I want to be a part of this."

It's obvious that when creating CTO, the Laws decided that they didn't just want to create an experience for their patients — they also wanted to create an experience for their team members. They knew this would only happen if they focused on the operational aspect of the business.

In the previous section, we broke down how to create a culture. CTO has definitely done that. But culture alone does not make a powerful and ultimately hugely successful practice. CTO understands that the operations side of the business is just as important to their success.

Average companies do one of two things when focusing on operations. They copy what seems to work for everyone else when it comes to the systems and flow of the office, or they hire a consultant to tell them what to do (which in the end produces the same result as the first, with maybe a few minor variations).

Extraordinary companies, the ones who find the most success, like Apple, Southwest Airlines and Airbnb, take a different approach than the rest.

In order to make operations most productive and create a unique experience people actually talk about, or in today's social media language, make it "go viral", they understand the three keys to creating outstanding company operations.

1. They hire their team based upon their individual "*Why.*"

2. They develop new and innovative systems.

3. They give the right responsibilities to the right people.

In the following section, you will learn how focusing on these three simple steps in the operation of your business will take your company from being "average" to extraordinary.

YOUR WHY

● ●

"There are two great days in a person's life –
the day they were born and the day we find out why."

— *William Barclay*

Hiring From *Why*

In order to know what you expect from yourself, you must first know what your *Why* is in life. What drives you to be your best? What makes you want more and want to do more? This is also true for your team. Earlier I spoke of the idea that the systems and flow of your business are the result of hiring correctly. When you have a group of people who come to work every day because they are living from their *Why*, better systems and a smooth workflow are the obvious result.

An office assistant in a chiropractic office was happy and doing well at her job. The doctor she worked for had hired me to come in and do some personal coaching with him and his team. Every quarter, I would go and do a specific training for that office based on the CORE concepts in this book. On the very first visit, I trained the entire team on the importance of knowing your *Why*. One by one, we dove into what makes each one of them tick and what makes them feel the most passionate.

At the end of the exercise, they had all stood and declared what their *Why* was. This team member revealed that her *Why* was making people happy. It seems simple enough, but her passion for this was so real that her #1 desire in life was to be Snow White at Disneyland. She just loved helping and caring for people and making them feel great. If she could do that every day for the rest of her life, she would.

The doctor took the training to heart and saw an opportunity. She was doing a fine job answering phones and assisting in the back office. But was she being used to her highest and best ability according to her *Why*? The doctor decided to perform an experiment.

Based on his new information about her *Why*, the doctor decided he wanted to assign her to a brand-new position in the office — and he made her his new customer experience coordinator.

When she asked him what the title meant, his honest answer was that he didn't exactly know. The only requirement was for her to take care of all clients that came through the door, to walk around the office and make people happy by making sure everybody was getting exactly what they wanted from the services available.

Her new title came with a new responsibility. She was to create the new expectations and then relay them to the doctor so that he could confirm that they fell in line with his vision and goals.

He reported that the difference in the way she approached her job was immediately different.

The doctor did the same exercise with everyone else in the office. Based on the role they were hired for, he took the *Why* they expressed and figured out a way to make sure that every single person in that office was working from their *Why* as closely as possible.

This can seem rather silly and petty, but the difference was definitely not.

Small shifts make a huge difference.

When your team works from their *Why*, they have a heightened sense of purpose and excitement. Think about what it would mean to live everyday knowing you were making a difference not only in your life, but the lives of others as well. You cannot do that unless you know your *Why*.

So, what exactly do I mean when I talk about your *Why*?

Some people call it your "calling." Others say it's your "come from." Garrett Gunderson calls it your "Soul Purpose."

Whatever you want to call it, I simply describe it as this:

The internal motivator that makes you the happiest in life.

It is the driving force behind what you do (or want to do) with your life. It's not usually about your labels like mom, spouse or your job title. It's much deeper than that.

Have you had a moment when someone in your life told you to find the one thing that you love to do so much that you would do it for free the rest of your life, if you could? Whatever that thing is, that is your *Why*.

Think about the positivity your office would have if everyone was working in their positions because that work was what they feel most passionate about in life, rather than working for a paycheck or the convenience. Knowing a potential employee's *Why* is a powerful tool when filling positions in your business.

In a TED talk (a group of inspirational talks given in under 20 minutes that are put together all over the country), speaker and author Simon Sinek talked about the reason why some companies are more successful than others. It's because they have figured out how to work from their *Why*.

But it goes beyond companies. The Wright Brothers, Dr. Martin Luther King Jr., and a plethora of others all found their ultimate success and changed the world because of their *Why*.

Sinek gives the example of Apple as a company that works specifically from their *Why*. It is not about what they do, who they are, or even the products they produce. (I highly recommend you look up that video on YouTube and watch it.)

In order to work from your *Why*, you need to find it first.

How do you find your why and how do you help others find theirs?

Well, I have an exercise that will let you to do just that.

If you know your *Why*, the How will work itself out!

Let me give you a few examples of a *Why*:
- "I believe in continual learning and gaining knowledge."
- "I want to be a care giver to others."
- "We believe there is a faster, better way to get results."
- "I'm passionate about helping kids overcome abuse."
- "I love to make people feel great!"

Exercise: Your *Why*

First, close your eyes and think of a time where you felt the most "you."

This is a time when you just felt like life was flowing in the direction you desired. It could have been in your childhood, adolescence or as an adult. It could have been a long period of time or just a short moment.

Focus on that moment.

Write down a short synopsis of that experience:

Now, answer the following questions. Dig deep with these answers and don't edit yourself. There is no right or wrong answer. Be willing to take your time.

1. **What makes you come alive? What inspires you?** *What makes you come alive isn't referring to taking your dream holiday or watching your favorite team play football, unless you're called to a career as a football coach or commentator. It's bigger than that!*

_____

_____

_____

_____

_____

_____

_____

_____

2. **What are your innate strengths?** *Where and when are you most in your element? Think about the things you've always been good at, sometimes perhaps wondering why others find them so hard.*

---

3. **Where do you add the greatest value?** *What problems do you really enjoy solving, and what problems do you feel passionate about trying to solve?*

---

4. **As a child, what did you want to be when you grew up?** *Think deeper than "fireman" or "princess." Look back at the people you admired and who they were, what they did.*

_____

_____

_____

_____

_____

_____

_____

_____

5. **If you had all the time and money in the world, what would you do?** *After all the travel and play died down, what is it that you would want to contribute, and would feel at bliss doing?*

_____

_____

_____

_____

_____

_____

_____

_____

_____

_____

6. **What drives you?**

_____

_____

_____

_____

_____

_____

_____

_____

_____

7. **What wakes you up every morning?**

_____

_____

_____

_____

_____

8. **When are you the happiest?**

_____

_____

_____

_____

_____

_____

_____

_____

9. In what areas do you feel the most creative?

_____

_____

_____

_____

_____

_____

10. What does an ideal working environment look like to you?

_____

_____

_____

_____

_____

_____

_____

_____

11. What hobbies or interests do you have that could potentially cross over into your responsibilities at work?

_____

_____

_____

_____

_____

_____

12. What activities drain your energy the most?

_____

_____

_____

_____

_____

_____

_____

_____

_____

13. If you could work from any place, any feeling in your life, if you could do anything you wanted for the rest of your life, or if you could position yourself somewhere in the office that would motivate you every day because of something that you felt passionate about, what would that be?

_____

_____

_____

_____

_____

_____

_____

Now, look at your answers and find a common theme(s) or thread.

What's the theme? If you can't find the specific theme, what are a few keywords that keep coming up? (Examples: fun, teach, learn, play, family, mother, caring, helping, etc.)

_____

_____

_____

_____

_____

_____

Is there anything in the answers you gave and the story you thought of that correlate? Think beyond just the obvious and see if there are any connections.

_____

_____

_____

_____

_____

_____

List the times where your theme or keywords have made an impact on your life.

_____

_____

_____

_____

_____

_____

List the times where the lack of your theme or keywords threatened your life, made you uneasy, made you feel unsafe or clouded your next move in life.

_____

_____

_____

_____

_____

_____

The "theme" is the basis of your *Why*.

The first step is to know what your *Why* is. Make sure you know from each of your team members what their *Why* is and if they are actually in the best position at work, based on their *Why*.

If you want a team that is positive and cohesive, find out what everyone's individual *Why*. Find out what they are best at, their individual *Whys*, and work from that.

What's Your Team's *Why's?*

Sit each team member down and ask them to think about these questions for awhile. Access the PDF version of this exercise and much more by getting access to The Path to the Propreneur at thepracticecure.com.

As the owner of your business, I hope you are working from your *Why*. If not, you need to shift your business practices to make sure that you are. For Scott and Jessica, their *Why* encompasses having fun, being exciting and not boring, being the best and most unique, standing out from the crowd, and not being afraid to push some boundaries.

They are successful because they work from their **Why**. It causes a ripple effect that extends to their team members, then to their clients. It makes success simple.

A group of people who only work for you for a paycheck, with no passion behind what they are doing, is the fastest way to a cookie-cutter, generic office.

When you have a group of people that actually focuses on their *Why's* and works from it, they will always give you their best.

Chapter Takeaway:

- In order to know what you expect from yourself, you must first know what your **Why** is in life.

- Your **Why** is the internal motivator that makes you the happiest in life. It is the driving force behind what you do (or want to do) with your life.

- The positivity in your office increases significantly when everyone works in their position from their **Why**, not because of a paycheck or convenience.

- When you work from your **Why**, you find success in your business and develop a greater personal satisfaction.

SYSTEMS

● ●

"For a business to survive and thrive, 100% of all the systems must be functioning and accountable. For example: An airplane is a system of systems. If an airplane takes off and the fuel system fails, there often is a crash. The same things happen in business. It's not the systems that you know about that are the problem — it's the systems you are not aware of that cause you to crash."

— Robert Kiyosaki, The Cashflow Quadrant

"If you can't describe what you are doing as a process, you don't know what you're doing."

— W. Edwards Deming, Total Quality Management

Joe Polish started off as a carpet cleaner in Arizona and now is a world-renowned marketing expert who coaches the likes of Arianna Huffington, Tim Ferriss, Tony Robbins and many more. Joe teaches that there are three stages to the purchasing process that every business needs to set up for their customers. Simply put, phase one is before the sale (the marketing), phase two is during the sale (the service given), and phase three is after the sale (the follow-up).

The greatest businesses in the world make sure that they are in as much control over all three of these experiences as possible. We will not go into detail about how to measure your results in this book, but it is a large part of my individual coaching program. Most mediocre companies only measure one or two of these areas. The exceptional companies make sure to consistently measure all three.

For the most part, the same steps should be utilized for every client or potential client who comes in contact with your business. These systems assure that you can actually measure the results accurately, only changing when the measurements warrant them.

In my experience, I have found that if you are struggling with client referrals, treatment plan acceptance rates, accounts receivable or client morale, I would be willing to bet it is due to a breakdown in (or lack of) systems.

To maximize the likelihood of clients investing in your services, from the moment somebody calls into the office, through their visit and until the moment they leave, there should be systems in place to make sure you know exactly what's happening in each specific area of your business.

Have you ever ordered a sandwich from Subway? They have now taken over McDonald's as the largest fast food chain in the country, so it's a good chance you have.

Subway is an excellent example of a specific system that is used every time, without fail. There are dozens of different ways you could make a sandwich, but not at Subway. Subway has systems for exactly how you order, and how they make your food. Go outside the system, and it throws everything off.

Notice how I mentioned that Subway is now the largest "fast food" restaurant in the world. Did calling Subway a fast food restaurant seem a bit odd to you? Most people don't think of Subway in the same category of fast food as McDonald's. It's a sandwich shop, not a greasy food joint. That is exactly what Subway wants you to think, and they've created a branding system that gives you the sense of making a better, more healthy choice when you pass by the large, bright yellow sign on your lunch hour. From the "Eat Fresh" tag line to professional athletes touting their "healthy" praises, Subway has created a system that makes you feel good about going to a fast food restaurant.

Now I'll illustrate two examples of companies who looked at what are "normal" systems in their profession and figured out a way to improve upon them. Some people look at these systems as radical and even question their ability to deliver the best service. Others use the excuse that it couldn't work in their business or town. I'm only using these systems as examples of how the owners changed things up to get new and dramatically better results.

A common practice in the orthodontic world when it comes to asking for referrals from their patients, if they do it at all, is to reward the referring patient with one of two options. They either enter patients into a drawing for some prize (the most popular being a digital tablet or a phone), or they are given a gift card to a local store or restaurant, usually in the amount of about $25.

Let me ask you this: When was the last time that $25 to a restaurant or the *chance* to win an electronic device actually motivated you enough to refer your friends and family to your doctor?

Of course, the hope is that your patients will refer you based on your great work and the stellar service you provide. However, a little more motivation never hurt. What if that motivation came in the form of cash in their pocket?

Now, before we get all worried about referral fee laws and such, keep reading and see how one of the most popular companies in the country has used this to their advantage.

The electric car company Tesla is gaining more and more popularity by the month. Waiting lists are being formed in order to buy one of these electric driving machines and, for the most part, it's not due to an environmental statement. It's due to a genuine love for the car and a desire to share it with friends and family due to a huge incentive from Tesla.

Tesla knows the importance of referrals. Since they don't do any advertising, marketing or product placement, they have to rely on it. If you see a picture of a celebrity in a Tesla, it's because the celebrity genuinely loves the car. If you see a Tesla in a movie or a TV show, it's because the production company genuinely loves the car.

In order to generate a desire for their customers to want to share their product with others beyond their personal satisfaction, they have created an outstanding incentive program. Each owner is given a unique hyperlink to the Tesla Motor Company website. That hyperlink is connected to the owner and has a deadline for sometime within the next 6 months. For every person that the customer refers to Tesla with the personal link and buys a car, the owner will receive a $1,000 credit towards service, merchandise, or *another* car. Then, the new buyer also receives an automatic $1,000 discount on their new car. The referring owner can receive up to 10 credits within the time frame required. That one customer has a potential to earn up to $10,000 worth of credit just for sharing Tesla!

Tesla has definitely shown this is enough to motivate a whole lot of people.

How can this principle work for you? What if you did the exact same thing?

For every new client that starts your services, they could receive a substantial credit to their account. Then, the new client also gets a credit for their new service.

One very important part of Tesla's referral program that most offices don't do, but definitely adds a sense of urgency to it, is the deadline. Don't leave your program open-ended. Clients are typically more prone to sharing their excitement with others at the beginning and the very end of their service. Give them a deadline of a few months from their start date.

I recently suggested to one of my orthodontists that they model the Tesla example for their referral program. They would give a $250 credit to each patient who refers a friend or family member who starts their treatment, maxing out at 10 referrals. They have a four month deadline until the incentive expires. The new patient would also receive a $250 credit to the purchase of their braces.

A new patient has the opportunity to bank up to $2,500 off the investment of their treatment. With the average cost of braces in the country being around $5,000, that is half off the cost. If the family has multiple children, this would be a huge incentive. For you, as the practitioner, those 10 referrals add up to $50,000 of new business. Would you invest $2500 in order to get a $50,000 return?

In the orthodontic world, Smile Doctors is the king of what is called "same-day starts." This means that they strive to start the actual orthodontic treatment by putting braces on a patient's teeth the first time he or she comes into the office. The first visit can, in many cases, mean that patients walk out with braces on and treatment started.

In many offices, patients go through a full examination, x-rays are taken, a work-up / write-up is completed and then patients are given the suggested plan from the doctor. If they say yes to the plan, a new appointment is scheduled for a few weeks later to have the braces placed. Some offices even schedule three appointments with the first one being just a visual check that does not include records before the actual transaction is made.

Even the suggestion of same day starts to some practitioners is met with disdain. Some are concerned the quality of service is lost, and others might not have the ability to schedule the time. I work with offices that see the benefit to this practice and others who flat out don't. I also work with a few offices that would like to implement it but know it is going to take a transition in both their mindsets as well as their schedules.

Smile Doctors decided that the normal process of taking weeks until delivery of the actual service was a waste of not only their time and efforts, but also that of the patient. They wanted to get patients excited about the process and give them a result right away, instead of hoping they would stay excited. They understood, from a sales point of view, that the longer the patient had to think about a procedure and get other quotes, the higher the likelihood they had of losing the patient. So why not give the patient what he or she wants and increase the opportunity to say yes by shortening the process?

In order to deliver this, they had to create multiple new systems throughout the patient process. One of the most important systems was offering the same-day start without it feeling pushy or rushed.

When someone calls the office to schedule an initial consultation, once the introduction is complete, the office team member plants a few seeds about getting the braces on the day the patient shows up for the first appointment, and simply says, "So if things go well, and the doctor thinks you are a good candidate, we can get your braces on the same day you come in."

And that theme of "We can get your braces on the same day you come in" continues throughout the entire experience. This mindset and verbal confirmation gears up each potential patient to accept the treatment coordinator's offer. They are creating a culture of sales in the company.

CTO doesn't focus on the "what if they can't afford it" or the "we need time to create a treatment plan" mentality that most offices do. They realize they are the doctors who have the prescription for the patient in need. They make sure their appointments are thorough and right for the client, and then present an opportunity for the client to get the immediate satisfaction he or she is looking for.

From a sales perspective, I love it. I think it's genius. And as a patient, I would be grateful that the doctor is not wasting my time.

For some scarcity-focused practices, this system may seem inappropriate and appalling, but the numbers speak for themselves. I would even venture to guess that some of you reading this example are thinking of all the reasons the same-day start method does not work for you. That is okay. That is not what I want you to focus on. The system CTO has created for same-day starts is just an *example* of a sales process they've found works well for them.

The main point is to strengthen the sales process for your business. I am confident in saying that if you are not focused on strengthening the sales process in your office, I would bet that you are struggling to hit your goals (assuming you are setting them in the first place).

Because the Laws decided not to get caught up in allowing other peoples' systems determine their business' fate, they have one of the highest same-day start ratios in the country.

After describing this example to one of my chiropractic clients when talking about systems, he wanted to share a personal example and how it affected his relationship with another professional.

"Let me tell you a story of what happened to me with my orthodontist, and how close that example hits home.

Taking one day off from my practice is roughly a $10,000 to $15,000 a day loss, but I knew I needed to get braces. I had waited long enough.

So in anticipation of getting braces, I scheduled my appointment with the only orthodontist in town and took a day off. I got the examination. I got the whole workup, and the orthodontist told me exactly what would happen.

I said, 'Great! Let's get started,' and pulled out my credit card.

He responded, 'Oh no. Today is just an initial consultation. We'll set another day for you to come in and get your braces.'

I go, 'But I scheduled my day off today in order to get the braces. I am sold. I'm ready.'

The orthodontist explained: 'We are not set up to start you today. I have to write up a treatment plan. We can get you in for that appointment in a few weeks.'

'You mean I have to take **another** day off? That's another $10,000 loss! So for my braces, which will cost me a total of about $6,000, I have to waste two $10,000 days?'"

He got up, walked out of the office and never returned.

That potential patient has likely talked about the experience to more than just me. He's talked about it to everybody in his office, to friends, and family members. Their system was, "We don't do same-day starts." If you cater to the world of professional practice owners, and maintain a flawed system, you'll lose out on not only one patient, but also any referrals.

A few things to take away from that story:

1. **Continually reexamine your systems to check their effectiveness.** Things change over time. Just because you have been doing things a certain way in your office for a long period of time doesn't mean you can't reexamine systems to see if they still make sense.

2. **Look for overlooked holes in your systems.** The system in the example above was broken, first and foremost, because the chiropractor was not told ahead of time that no actual placing of braces happens the day of the appointment.

3. **When someone is offering you money for your services now, take it now.** Isn't making money one of the reasons you are in business?

In a moment I will talk about how you can satisfy the client even if you don't give them the full service right away.

It's important to examine the systems you currently have and decide if they are causing you to lose money for no particular reason, and if they can be expanded upon, or if they can be reworked altogether.

While visiting Dr. Datwyler's office in Sacramento, I was able to show him a twist on his system that would immediately up his bottom line.

Whenever I visit an office, I will focus the majority of my time with the person in charge of sales. This is the most important position in any company. If you don't have sales, you are just engaging in a hobby. You are not in business. As I mentioned in the previous example, in an orthodontic office, this responsibility falls on the head of the Treatment Coordinator (TC for short).

In my normal fashion, I made sure to visit the TC's office and sit in on a few patient consults she had that day. From a previous conversation with Dr. D, I already knew that due to scheduling and space, performing same-day starts was not a focus in their office.

As I sat in on two of the presentations made by the TC, I saw a recurring theme. After Dr. D went over the proposed treatment plan, he politely excused himself and the TC would continue by pulling out the payment options according to the potential patient's insurance. She would explain how much the patient would be responsible for and how much the insurance would cover. Then she explained the cash price and what the payment arrangements would look like, if they were needed. She would then tell the potential patient that their first payment would not have to be made until after impressions were taken, either during the second or third visit. Then, she wisely asked when would be a good time to schedule the next visit. They scheduled the follow up appointment for the next available slot six weeks away and the patient exited. It was a good system and she had it down.

Do you see the major mistake here? Do you see the opportunity missed?

To give this TC credit, she was actually great at things like assuming the sale and getting them on the schedule right away. She was very good at answering questions, empathizing, and resolving any concerns. (Let me be clear that my goal here is not to throw this TC under the bus. It is just to point out how to look at a potential system in a business that might be working, but is not benefiting your business.)

I could talk about the fact that, for the most part, doctors should not have to be in the room to educate the client on what the process is going to be. In an efficient office, the doctor is only needed to confirm what the TC has explained, but that's another topic.

What I did not mention was that in both the presentations I sat in, the potential patients were the one to confirm when the first payment was due. One person even reached into her purse to grab her wallet when the TC said, "Not until the second visit" in an assuring tone.

This is where the same-day start mentality can help add immediate money into the business. Even if the patient is not physically getting braces on her teeth today, there is still a start that *mentally* needs to happen.

The same-day start model works well because it taps into the patient's desire for immediate satisfaction. This is what you have to give your clients to secure the sale. In the client's mind, putting down money shows that the ball is rolling and there is immediate action towards solving the problem. Making an appointment or signing a contract does not hold the same value. The transaction happens in a client's mind when money is exchanged.

If the parents and patient leave the office without putting any money down, then have to wait 4-8 weeks until the next appointment, the parent has anywhere from 1-2 months to change their mind. That is plenty of time for little Johnny's mom to hear from little Johnny's best friend's mom how much the family loves "Dr. So and So" across town, and then decide to get an exam from him, and potentially change her mind about the appointment. However, if a transaction had taken place with you, in the mother's mind the treatment has already started and the odds of seeking another opinion are slim to none.

A crucial system that must be implemented in every office is a sales system that focuses on getting your clients to make a financial commitment before they leave the office. That gives you money in your business right now, versus the potential for money in the future (that is, if they actually show up for their next appointment).

Business success is not built on potential. It is built on profit.

When you have systems in place and a culture of sales is present, everyone on the team has a part to play in solidifying transactions. Here is a simple experiment for you to conduct. Tomorrow morning, gather your team around you for a quick meeting. Then ask the sales department to raise their hands. I would be willing to guess, based upon what I have seen, that you will get a good share of blank stares while your TC or hygienist and maybe your office manager raises their hands. (If your TC doesn't respond, you have a bigger problem.)

> Business success is not built on potential. It is built on profit.

When everyone on your team quickly raises their hands, you know you have created the culture of sales necessary for success.

Systems in your business are not just for the benefit of your clients; they are also for the benefit of your team and yourself. When your team knows what to expect on a daily basis, a sense of understanding, pride and accomplishment is established. Creating systems for every aspect of your business not only helps get rid of the headaches, but creates clarity. And clarity is power.

Obviously, systems are going to be different for every individual company. Let me give you a few examples of possible systems in hope of kick-starting ideas. Then, I will give some specific examples of how other companies have used systems for their success.

SYSTEMS BEFORE

1. Separate yourself from competition.

Do you know the difference between Apple's Mac computer and a PC? Both products are computers. They might have different operating systems and design features, but when you get down to it, there is not much you can't do on one that you can do on the other.

The difference is in the marketplace positioning.

Apple has done a better job of separating its products from the crowd through its marketing and message. They don't even view the PC as competition. They let the various brands under the PC label (Samsung, Hewlett Packard, Daewoo, Compaq, IBM, etc.) fight it out amongst themselves with pricing, design and features. Apple lives in its own computer universe, if you will, creating a top quality product, at a top tier price tag, and creating a movement around just about anything they create.

You can and *must* do the same. It's imperative for you to create a unique brand that creates a movement around what you do and pay no attention to the so-called competition in your area. If you are worried about the other professionals who do what you do in your town, then you are just another "PC" doctor trying to gain customers based upon price, location and convenience.

However, when you become the specialist in your area by becoming "The Whole Health Clinic" instead of a chiropractor's office or "The Smile Architect" instead of Dr. G, DDS, you can start to create your own Apple-like movement in your industry.

How do you do this, you ask? The first step is to build up your vision and your core values. Now let's go deeper.

133

Write down 5 ways you can separate yourself from the "others" out there who do what you do.

1. _____
2. _____
3. _____
4. _____
5. _____

2. Create value-based advertising with a call-to-action.

99% of professional practice advertising is simply a different version of the competition's advertising. They provide the basic information: company name, phone number, website and a weak plead like "Call us today." They think they are standing apart from their competition because they have a nicer-looking family in their ad, brighter colors or a cooler logo.

Don't just tell them who you are and what you do. Everyone is doing that. Set yourself apart by giving them value right now without anything in return. (And no, a free consultation doesn't count!)

One of the fastest ways to set yourself apart as an expert in your field is to educate the customer on something they should be aware of in your industry, via a report, consumer guide, or even a book.

In order to truly stand out, you have to do something different. When you provide potential clients with specific information that helps them solve a problem they have, you automatically position yourself in their minds as someone who provides value to their lives, and as the expert in your field.

Instead of using generic ad copy, invite them to get your free report on the topic you choose right now by calling in, logging on or texting their information to you. The only thing you ask in return is that they give you a way to deliver it, their contact information, i.e. address, email, name or phone number. It's the fastest and best way to make them engage with you — by compelling them to virtually raising their hands to say, "I am interested in what you have."

It's easy to do, valuable because it converts more people, shows you are the expert and most importantly... it's measurable. You can actually measure what your ROI is on your marketing by how many people are asking for your report.

Here are a few examples of topics you could easily write about.

- "The top 5 things you need to know before you get your kids braces"

- "What your dentist is not telling you"

- "10 common mistakes accident victims make when dealing with their insurance company"

Make it known that YOU are the expert... Today!

To create your own report, follow along with a simple walkthrough at thepracticecure.com. You'll find a done-for-you template to help you create an expert positioning report that will make your clients recognize **you** as the expert.

---

3. Utilize the "on hold" recording to promote the practice, not your resume.

Obviously, we don't want potential clients to hear a recorded message, but it's going to happen sometimes. Instead of playing music on the line, play pre-recorded "congratulations" messages touting recent patient wins. These serve as social proof to potential clients, and affirm to current clients that they've made a great decision.

Here are a couple good examples:

"Congratulations to Sally from Bonneville Middle School who was able to get her braces off 5 months early due to her excellent treatment of her braces."

"We'd like to announce our newest members of the Dynamic Dental family. The Smith family from Hayes joined our Smile Club for just $18 a month and now are getting 20% off annual cleanings for the entire family."

You could really have a great time with this one. Those types of messages can also easily be consistently updated on your website for the same result.

4. Special first-time caller call-in numbers.

Use a specific number in your advertising that rings to a specific area in your office for new clients. If possible, equip the phone with caller ID and make sure each caller is greeted in a unique manner. Imagine how impressed the client will be to hear this:

"Hi, is this Ms. Johnson? We are thrilled you contacted us today. I'm excited to make your first conversation with us worth your while. How can I best help you today?"

You can also add something similar by using a special code or having special line ring based on the number in your advertisement.

SYSTEMS DURING

1. Greeting the Client

Are you just calling out the next client's name when it's their turn, or are you physically walking over to her, stating her name, offering your hand in recognition, then guiding her to the back while engaging in a conversation with her? What would make them feel more appreciated and welcomed... even if it's their tenth time at the office?

2. Progress Charts

Have your clients personally write their progress and goals based on your treatment plan and have them bring it to every appointment. This makes them an active participant in your treatment goals. Each time they bring it in, an assistant reviews it and signs it off. After benchmarks are hit, they gain something of value, are added in a special raffle, or given a prize. If you are really tech savvy, you could make it an online program or an app. Research has shown that gamification ultimately leads to more participation and, ultimately, more success.

3. Daily Team Meeting

Average companies hold morning meetings once in a while. That is **not** a system. A system is a habit for your business that helps you stay informed. Daily team meetings set up an attitude of success for that day and beyond. Extraordinary practices hold a morning meeting every day.

Daily morning meetings help your team align with the goals of the day, recognize and celebrate the accomplishments from yesterday, coordinate how to deal with challenging clients coming to visit that day, and gain awareness of other special announcements, events, or procedures.

So much power comes from holding daily morning meetings. It makes sense to incorporate them in to your business.

Your clients will feel the difference in the camaraderie, the coordination and the attention to detail that morning meetings create, even though they are not there to see it.

You could come up with a laundry list of reasons why your business is special and doesn't need morning meetings. I've heard them all before. Most of your reasons and excuses probably have to deal with either time or money, both of which are perfectly fine reasons... if you want to be just an average practice and don't want to see massive results in your office culture.

I have yet to hear from an office that decided to invest the time and money into productive daily meetings that the team did not experience an increase in productivity, creativity and all-around performance in the office. Daily morning meetings are a system every company with a team needs.

4. Special Referral Card

Give all current clients a unique or special referral card to share when they want to send a friend your way. Have it reward both the user and the giver with a special gift (movie discounts, entry in a raffle, meal coupon) that's activated when the referral calls in and makes an appointment.

SYSTEMS AFTER

1. Accepted Treatment Celebration

Ever notice that many of the Best Buy stores have their customers pick up their merchandise in the front of the store? They do this for two reasons: 1) To give the big purchaser an opportunity to mentally show off what they just bought, and 2) so that those that haven't made a purchase yet will see others making the choice and maybe get a bit envious of them, thus giving them the extra push through social proof to buy.

When someone accepts treatment, do you make it a big deal? You can take them out to the main area and introduce him/her to your entire team as your newest patient. This allows them to feel special.

2. Follow-up call

Are you or someone within the team calling the patient the evening after their treatment to see how they are doing? At a minimum, you could send an email or a text to let them know you care.

3. Follow-up packet

You can send them a special care kit after the initial treatment with simple suggestions for comfort, or things to be aware of. It doesn't have to be anything fancy. Then you can offer a more simple item after follow-up visits. These can include marketing pieces about referrals, contests and even upcoming events. What can you do to impress them when they are no longer in the office?

Systems are needed in every area of your business.

What are your systems? Do they make sense? Are they promoting your business and moving the ball forward when it comes to the success of your business, or are they hindering your true success? It's important to see that the system in Dr. Datwyler's office was "working" well enough in his and the TC's eyes, and if they'd continued to use it, they would have probably been fine. The goal, however, is to implement systems that are not just getting by, but are major needle-movers.

Creating systems that actually move you toward success is the key factor in creating efficient operations.

Be willing to critique your system. Not all systems are good, just like we have seen. Some systems are just bad habits. Most are ones you picked up from other people in your same profession. The timeworn adage *"if it isn't broke, don't fix it"* doesn't fly if you are looking to take your business to the next level. You must be willing to implement specific, driven systems in your business. This will lead to sure success.

Here are some of the systems you might want to review in your business.

- New client intake process
- Sales
- Marketing
- Advertising
- Team meetings
- Celebrating successes
- Sponsorships
- Referral requests
- Team member time or days off

What are some areas of your business that you are already starting to recognize that you might want to take another look at? Use the space below to write them down.

_____

_____

_____

_____

_____

_____

In order to boost morale and start the day off positively with your morning meetings, add these simple exercises:

- **Recite / review your core values.** (Either one person at a time or the entire group at once.) Undercover Boss star and CEO of the Dwyer Group, Dina Dwyer, implemented this rule not just for her direct companies but also as part of the agreement for any franchise owner. Why? So that everyone was always clear on the importance of the company's core values. What a great way to start the day.

- **Ask an empowering rhetorical question every day.** What if you ended the meeting with a question for everyone to reflect on all day like, "How can we do more?", "What am I doing to impress them?" or "Am I acting from my highest self?"

- **Celebrate small successes.** We will talk about this more in the final section, Excellence, but start thinking now about ways that you can quickly celebrate the small everyday successes that your team achieves.

- **Company cheer.** Start the day off with a "We can do this!" cheer. If you have clients waiting in the lobby, let them hear it. When they know that the people about to assist them in their treatment are excited and motivated, it can be magical.

Need a systems overhaul?

For more examples and sales training, from how to get the right information over the phone to how to set up for the close, sign up for The Path to the Propreneur at thepracticecure.com.

Chapter Takeaway:

- There are three phases to the buying process that need systems in place. Phase one is before the sale (the marketing), phase two is during the sale (the service given), and phase three is after the sale (the follow-up).

- Creating systems for every aspect of your business not only helps get rid of the headaches, but it creates clarity. Clarity is power.

- Business success is not built on potential; it is built on profit. When you have those systems in place and a culture of sales is present, everyone on the team has a part to play in solidifying the transaction.

- Continually reexamine the systems in place to ensure their effectiveness.

RESPONSIBILITIES

"The price of greatness is responsibility."

— *Winston Churchill*

While on a call with my client, he started telling me that the last two days had been tough — the computer system in the office had gone out and he was having a hard time fixing it. He heard the shock in my voice as I said, "Excuse me? Are you a computer tech? (He was not.) Why are you working on the computer system when you should be focused on your patients?"

He sounded as if he was apologizing as he started to tell me that he was pretty good with computers normally, and that no one else in the office could do it, so he just decided to jump in and fix it.

I asked his permission to be blunt. He chuckled a bit as if he already knew what I was going to say.

I politely but firmly said, "You are not a computer technician. For two days now, your office has been running at a less than ideal capacity, not because of the computers being down, but because you are not willing to hand off the responsibility of fixing the computers to the professionals. That is not only terrible business practice — it's bad leadership to your team."

There was a moment of silence before he said, "I know, you're right. I'll call someone to come in tomorrow and fix it."

As a business owner you have to be willing to hand over the responsibilities of things you are not a genius at (anything you don't get paid the most to do) to those who are. If you don't have the genius in your office, find him or her.

When team members are not crystal clear on their individual responsibilities, this causes confusion. As I said before, the confused mind says no. So, make sure that everyone's responsibilities are clearly laid out, and the systems will support the responsibilities that are given.

It is your responsibility as a leader to delegate.

Good leaders empower their teams as individual members to achieve more. Delegating tasks does just that. In doing so, you are able to take the burden of little tasks off your plate for good.

Being in charge of a business is a lot like being a conductor of an orchestra. The conductor in no way tries to play every instrument. If he or she did, there would be no symphony. Instead, the conductor stands in front and leads the group, focusing on a few key aspects — the tempo, unifying the performers and molding the performance by listening to every player. There are a handful of things that the conductor can do that no one else can do, and it involves stepping back to view the big picture with critical ears and eyes.

Task Breakdown

The first step in delegation requires that you understand how the office works and knowing exactly what is needed to make the office run. Many people think they know what it takes, but making a list of tasks may lead to some surprising realizations.

Start by making a list of every task required for your business to operate smoothly. Remember to think of more than just daily tasks!

What does it take to run your business at every level? Marketing, advertising, networking, supply ordering, etc. Brainstorm with your team if necessary. This is not just a good exercise for this part of the book, but it's also a great resource if you have to replace someone. When you have a binder of exactly what tasks are necessary and exactly whose responsibility they are, then you have peace of mind knowing you can easily replace a vacant position.

Tasks Required for My Business to Run Smoothly: (Place a special mark next to the things you have to do. If you run out of room, get out some paper and write a complete list.)

1. _____
2. _____
3. _____
4. _____
5. _____
6. _____
7. _____
8. _____
9. _____
10. _____
11. _____
12. _____
13. _____
14. _____
15. _____
16. _____
17. _____
18. _____
19. _____

20. _____

21. _____

22. _____

23. _____

In a company overview, a client revealed to me his concern about his finance manager. Not about her as a person, but that he actually didn't know exactly what she does and how she does it.

"If she ever leaves me, I don't have a clue to most of what she does. It stresses me out."

I bet it did. I told him he immediately needed to get her an assistant that she could teach so that he could have a backup. Guess what happened two months later? Yep, she was moving and put in her two weeks notice. It was a good thing he already had the new assistant in place.

The point is, even though it is your practice, there is no way you know how to do everything that needs to be done, and, to the point of this chapter, you shouldn't have to. You're the conductor.

Once you have the list, start breaking the tasks down by department, then specific team members whose purview that task would be under. If there is no one specifically assigned to a task or you are not sure, put it in a different column under To Be Assigned. For example, if no one is quite sure about who is in charge of marketing, then that would go under the "To Be Determined" column.

Now comes the hard part for many of you — actually finding out what your job is and what it is not.

Your 3 Things

Chances are, you're taking on more work than you should, albeit out of old habits, the need for control, frustration or just plain superhero-ism. It's time to stop!

In order to be a great leader, you should only be doing three things. Everything else should be delegated to either your employees or hired-out help.

At a networking event, I met Dan Sullivan, the owner of Strategic Coaching. His company is incredibly successful and has trained companies around the globe for the last few decades. He spoke at the event about how important it is for business owners to focus on only the things that they are experts at and nothing else. He said that whenever he even thinks about doing anything outside of his genius circle (his three things), things get messed up in his business.

Honestly, I got it, but I also wanted to believe I was special and that I could bend the rule as long as it made sense to me.

As it so happened, on my way to lunch one day I ended up walking next to Mr. Sullivan, and I saw my opportunity to ask him a question about my special circumstance. In my rationalizing mind, he'd help my point and give me his blessing to break the one rule for success he just finished telling everyone to follow.

"Mr. Sullivan. I have a question about the three things," I said.

"Yes?" he responded.

"Although I agree and it makes sense, what do you do with those things that are right on the other side of your circle? The things that you want to do, even if you might not necessarily get paid to do them?"

He looked at me with a definitive glance, "I don't have those. I can't afford to. The moment I get distracted by the things that are not what I am best at, my business suffers." He continued, "Those things are not why I am in business, those things keep me from being my best at business. And if you are even dabbling in things that you are not being paid for, they are stopping your business from growing the way you want it to. I guarantee it."

I knew he was speaking the truth. I knew that I was just searching for an excuse to not follow the advice from someone who was more successful than me, hoping he would make an exception for my "special" case. Instead, he called me on it.

So now I am going to ask you to apply this style of leadership to your business. There are only three things you should be doing. These things are probably what you went through years of schooling for and are the only one qualified to do. You may be the only one legally able to perform the task. I would venture to guess that most of the stuff you do, you do out of habit, not necessity.

Let's look at one orthodontist as an example. This particular orthodontist laid out his three "rock star" responsibilities as:

- Treatment/diagnosis
- Implementation of treatment (braces on / braces off)
- Relationship building (Personal letters / phone calls to other doctors

The important point here is that only he can do them. Originally, he had four "must-do" tasks. In addition to with doctors, he had said that letters to patients was in his small circle. He was in the habit of writing them and figured it was easier for him to do it, not wanting to take the time to train his team. He also worried about their competency in the task. How could they write a letter like it was from him?

After some consideration, he realized that the return on investment for his time spent writing the letters was minimal. He could spend 30 days training a team member, reviewing each letter and giving constructive criticism and pointers. The return of investment would stay the same due to proper training. After those 30 days, writing letters to patients would no longer be on his to-do list, freeing his time and saving his energy.

Look at the list you created earlier. Now, really look at all the things you marked as the person who has to do it. Do you really have to do it or are you choosing to do it? If money were not an issue, would you still do it? If you are using personal feelings like "but I enjoy doing it" or "I want to do it," that is not a good enough reason for this exercise. You might not even know who could do it right now, but if it is not your direct genius, then it is not your responsibility.

It's time to find your circle of responsibility. Use the space on the next page to write down everything you do. In the small circle, write the three things ONLY YOU can do. In the outer circle list everything else you do, down to the tiniest of tasks.

Your brain is going to tell you that you should be doing more. It's time to challenge that way of thinking. Really push yourself. The point of this exercise is to really narrow it down. Say something happened and it was only possible for you to do three things. What would they be?

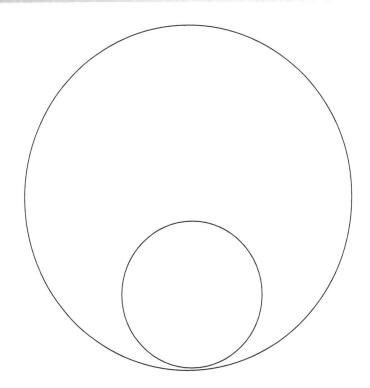

At this point, I'm sure you're wondering what you're supposed to do with all the other tasks you've taken on that are listed in the outer circle. It all boils down to delegation.

Use this section to list your three essential responsibilities. Everything else needs to be taken out of your circle! Delegation equals success.

My Three "Only Me" Responsibilities:

1. _____

2. _____

3. _____

The rest can be delegated. I did not say it was going to be easy, but I will tell you that the faster you take the work off your plate and find the right people to do those things, the more that will get done and the better your business will run.

The Difference Between Delegation and Abdication

WARNING!

There is no way to completely disengage from the tasks you delegate. If you do, you **are not** delegating. You are abdicating. You are still ultimately accountable for the outcome; therefore, you should still have a level of oversight. Your team is acting *on your behalf.* Proper delegation not only requires structure and forethought, it requires ongoing support and supervision. Complete abdication from responsibility is not only a lazy way to do business; it can also be dangerous to the business.

Recently, I've had cases of two doctors who have had to learn this lesson the hard way. One was a dentist from Kansas who admitted to not even knowing what his bank account number was. I was a little surprised and asked him what he meant, and he said to me that over the last twenty years of practice, he always let his bookkeeper and his wife take care of all the money. He didn't have anything to do with it because all he wanted to do was dentistry.

The challenge with that arrangement was that when it came down to it, he had no idea what was in the bank account. He was not being a good steward of his money, because he couldn't be. He actually had to guess what bank they banked with when I inquired.

The second situation is a little more intense. For the sake of my clients, I will call them George and Fiona. Both are orthodontists and have been in practice together for over 20 years. A few years ago, they found out that their entire retirement was taken from them via embezzlement by their in-house bookkeeper. The person was sweet, kind and you would have never thought she would do anything of that nature. Neither did George and Fiona. I am not suggesting that it's entirely George and Fiona's fault. I'm only pointing out that when we just give away the responsibility to avoid headaches, we open ourselves up to situations like this.

No matter how big your practice or business is, at the end of the day, you are the owner and you have a responsibility to take stewardship of it. Even Oprah has famously said that no matter how much money she's made and how many people are working for her, she still signs every check that goes out of her business to make sure she knows what's going on.

Exercise: Delegation

What are the tasks that you have no involvement or oversight in at this moment?

_____

_____

_____

_____

_____

_____

Why might it be important to have some level of oversight in the above tasks? What are possible consequences of a lack of oversight?

_____

_____

_____

_____

_____

Go deeper into delegation.

Download this activity for further walkthrough by accessing The Path to the Propreneur at **thepracticecure.com**.

Strengths, Weaknesses and Hidden Talents

Every person has something they truly excel at, something they struggle with and, most likely, a skill that makes them stand out from others. To build a rock star team, we must know each employee's strengths, weaknesses and hidden talents.

Just like in an orchestra, each person plays to his or her strengths. But say, for instance, a flute player has a hidden talent — he can blow any trombone player out of the water. Sure, he's competent on the flute, but the orchestra would have much more success if he were only playing the trombone.

You may say that in the real world, that would never happen. Why didn't that person audition for the correct position in the first place? Sometimes, all that matters to a player (or an employee) is getting a foot in the door. That person may think, "At least I'm in the orchestra. Maybe when the trombone player retires, I'll take over." There could be a thousand reasons why this person isn't playing the trombone. The point here is that there is a hidden talent that could really benefit the entire group, if only the conductor knew.

You may hire someone based on one talent but discover other talents later. Leaning upon and using your team's talents creates a certain type of culture in the office. It lets them know you care about not only the office's growth but also about growth on an individual level. When you explore their talents, your team feels anchored. They feel challenged. You may have to compensate them for their time, but it's well worth it, considering how happy and appreciated your team will feel when they know they're valuable to you.

Amy was a receptionist in Dr. A's office and did a great job. She was personable and easy to get along with, and everyone who came in was naturally attracted to her. She had a natural gift of persuasion as well. Upon discussion of hidden talents, we realized, with a little sales training, that Amy would make a natural treatment coordinator. She was willing to learn and within a few weeks, the office had a new and formidable treatment coordinator.

Every person will contribute something unique to your office. In order to tap into everyone's unique abilities, you must have conversations. Have an individual meeting with each person to discuss what he or she feels his or her strengths and weaknesses are. Most importantly, talk about any hidden talents they feel they have.

This is not necessarily your responsibility to do — after all, we're trying to take tasks off of your plate! Your office manager can handle this part perfectly well. Just be aware, though, of the skills and talents so you can fully utilize each person.

As a jumpstart, here are some potential questions to ask your team to get going:

- Are they a wiz at building an Excel spreadsheet?
- Do they have major proofreading skills?
- Were they in the math league in high school? Can they crunch numbers with ease?
- Do they have creativity pouring out of your fingertips?
- Can they organize like no other?
- Do they love throwing parties?

Using these questions and more, get together with your core team and start brainstorming ways to utilize these talents. Try and come up with at least two uses for each talent. Once you have information, don't be surprised if you find yourself looking for new and powerful ways to utilize these talents to grow your practice's culture.

Training Needs

Once you have broken down your responsibilities, your team's responsibilities, and have uncovered the bonus of knowing their hidden talents, there are three specific systems to create so that you can have a cohesive team roadmap and be a successful leader.

1. Create an Operations Manual

Now, use the list you created that contains every task required for a successfully run office. As part of a team exercise, have each person help list the essential steps required to perform each task on the list correctly. (Make sure you write down how often each task should be completed.) After the worksheet below is complete, compile all worksheets into a comprehensive operations manual. With this worksheet for reference, you now know what it takes for every task in your office to be completed correctly.

Below is a simple example of a task outline. I encourage you to use more detail in yours!

Task & Frequency:	**New Client Follow Up Process** *(Weekly)*
Step 1	Gather list of patients that visited x months ago.
Step 2	Make phone calls to each – "It's been awhile since we've seen you, just checking…"
Step 3	Send follow up email – remind that you've called, tell them to be on lookout for mail from office.
Step 4	Mail coupon / promotional material.

> **Creating your Operations Manual has never been easier.**
>
> Download and print as many Task Outlines as you need at thepracticecure.com.

2. Determine Training Needs

It's now time to decide who within your office needs to be trained for the tasks you're taking off your plate. Based on the strengths, weaknesses and hidden talents of your team, determine who you can delegate tasks to. Use this form to track each task that is being delegated and who is responsible for the training. Sign off on the completion date only when you're sure the task can be done correctly.

Task to Delegate	To Whom	Training Needs	Trainer	Completion Date
Holiday letters	Receptionist	Minimal – needs address list	Dr.	10/1

> Print off the Training Needs Form today!
>
> Make your life that much easier. Have all of the training needs for your entire team on one form. Because you'll be delegating a lot of tasks, it's important to know who has been given each task. Know the answers at a moment's notice! Access the official Training Needs Form at thepracticecure.com.

3. Cross Training Staff

Cross training ensures that no matter what the circumstances, there is someone on your team who can complete any task. Your team members become empowered and feel valued. Your office succeeds and has a minimal fail rate.

The cross-training log should be filled out for each team member. Make sure they know what they are being trained in, why they are being trained, and what your desired outcome is. Go through the resources that may be required and any arrangements that need to be made.

A very important aspect of comprehensive cross training involves knowing the necessary skills of the task and the competency of the task's performer. Since you've already completed the task outlines for your office, the skills needed should already be known. List the skills your team member needs to develop and estimate his or her starting ability. By the end of cross training, the goal is to have them at a level 5. Prioritize each task; some skills may be more necessary to master. Decide on a completion date and check in at the halfway point. Sign off on each skill only when employees are fully trained in it. After every skill has been mastered, fill out the bottom section and file the log in their employee file.

Down the line, it can be referred to if necessary.

Need help organizing the cross-training process?

Streamline the cross-training process by knowing the details. Paired with the other worksheets in this chapter, you'll have the tools you need to delegate properly. Download the cross-training log at thepracticecure.com.

You have laid out the foundation for an empowered team who fully understands their responsibilities. Congratulations!

Successful business operations only happen when everybody in the business is working from their *Why*, when they understand the systems that are in place, and when they are clear on their responsibilities. When you have these three things working together, your operation or business will not just be successful, but will be something that other practitioners in your space envy.

Chapter Takeaway:

- It is your responsibility as a leader to delegate. Good leaders empower their teams as individual members to achieve more. Delegating tasks does just that.

- When delegating tasks, make sure there is proper training and oversight. Do not abdicate!

- When everyone is clear on their responsibilities, both specific and general, you will find your team members will be better at managing themselves, and the need for oversight will be less necessary.

"When I was looking at a practice, I wanted to make sure that it was something where things were divided equally, where the patients were considered patients of the whole practice, not divided. Knowing that it's a group effort, that you are part of the team, and that everything is shared in that aspect is very important.

Something that I learned in the process is there are all different kinds of personalities. Now I can see what motivates other people. Once you take a look at that, it's very interesting in the office setting.

I know that if I work with Rachel over here, she really feeds off of personal praise when she's getting her work done. If I tell her she did a great job, it will make her day, but if I work with Sarah over here, she is more driven by reaching her goals for the day. The numbers drive her.

Knowing different personality types, what people feed off of, and how to communicate with them is something that is not necessarily intuitive to everybody, but knowing or even being able to recognize those is something that I'm still developing and I hope to develop even further.

But it's not something you ever really will sit down and just think about. Go out and read books or talk to coaches. It is an important skill set to develop."

Dr. Jenna Shevlin, DDS
Brilliant Smiles

SECRET BONUS CHAPTER: ALPHA V. BETA LEADERSHIP

In marriage mentoring, I talk about the importance of understanding the alpha and beta energy between husband and wife. Alpha is more dominant, while beta is more submissive. Both spouses can use the alpha and beta energy depending on the situation, but for the most part, we are biologically made up so that men utilize a bit more alpha and women a bit more beta. This is not a "men should be domineering and women should be submissive" thing. It's a "how do we biologically, naturally respond to each other" thing.

Some people have the misunderstanding that to be alpha means to be belligerent, rude and chauvinistic. Visions of a sweaty man in a white "wife beater" tank top come to mind. That is not the case.

Alpha, broken down to its simplest form, means being a leader. In today's society, many men are living in beta energy more often. This can be a good thing in that they are more sensitive, willing to share in responsibilities, and tap into their emotional side when necessary. It can also be a turnoff for a spouse over time. A man who is consistently in their beta does not cause the female to react well to him. It's not a turn on, if you will, and eventually she'll feel less secure. It's not that she doesn't like the emotional side. But at the same she also, biologically, wants to know that he is a leader and protector of her.

When challenges come up in the marriage and she expresses her concern by complaining about how things have changed, not really being able to put her finger on what it is, modern beta men tend to double down on the beta and become even less of the leader that the spouse is craving.

"Be a leader," she says. "Stop saying, 'I don't know' when asked simple questions, make the plans for the date, the weekend or the vacation, be consistent in the discipline of the children." When he does this, she gains respect, admiration and desire for him.

If he doesn't, she will eventually, if she has not already, start to take over that alpha position for her own feeling of security, and he then complains that she is always in control and never lets him make a decision.

Marriages that get to this point struggle to find a peaceful balance in the relationship unless they get the right help to point it out and work on ways to bring the balance back.

I point this out because for male-owned practices, I see the same situation in the office. Doctors frequently fade into beta and won't step into their alpha to be effective leaders. They do this partly due to the fact that no one ever taught them how to rely on alpha when needed, but also because, like the husband who doubles down on the beta hoping it will make his wife happy, they think it will be the fastest way to peace in the office.

Let's face it: your practice is like a marriage. And just like a marriage, you have to know how to balance the alpha and the beta in your business. In the case of most professional practices, there tends to be multiple "wives" to one or two "husbands." This can happen for practices owned by women too, but it's not as prevalent.

Typically, when I see an office experiencing challenges with understanding of responsibilities, too much gossip, disrespect of the owner and others, I ask the owner about quality of leadership. Due to the heavy female concentration of most teams, the doctor has become emasculated and has allowed the leadership role to be suppressed, not wanting to appear too Alpha.

Countless times, I have talked privately with male owners and asked how "in charge" they feel when it comes to office management, the ability to make policy or procedure decisions, or just all-around respect — and they admit to feeling like there is little or none.

This is not the fault of the team. This is the fault of the leadership. The owner doesn't want to come across as berating, demanding or controlling, so he is "Mr. Nice Guy," so much so that he lets little insubordinations or infractions happen without correction. Some examples could be consistently showing up late, leaving early, failing to fully implement the new training you have requested, pointing out an owner's mistake or flaw in a team meeting, needing time off without warning, undermining your orders to a client, disrespect to venders or consultants, gossip outside of work about your business, or creating conflict with other team members.

I hope you get the picture.

The biggest indicator of how emasculated an owner is comes in the form of body language.

In my work, understanding body language is vital to being able to ask better questions from my clients. Body language is a great way to see more of the story. I became certified in body language so that I could help clients at a deeper level. When evaluating an office, reading body language gives me an edge that most don't have. From seeing hidden signs of contempt via the eye movements of an a employee to watching the comfort or discomfort level of a client, body language is a great tool in creating better relationships that I think every office needs.

Although I do not believe that one "sign" always means one thing, (typically you need to read body language in clusters), there is a sign I always look for in an office that shows how emasculated the owner has become. It's called the Fig Leaf.

It's when the person stands with hands crossed in front, covering the crotch area, thus forming a "fig leaf" over the genitals. When I see this sign I typically have an owner who, for whatever reason, in that moment, is feeling emasculated.

Again, I would need to ask more questions and look at more interactions, but for the most part, I am pretty right on when it comes to this evaluation.

It will be harder, now that you are aware, but check in with yourself to see if you do the fig leaf in certain situations and in talking to certain people. You might think it's not a big deal but if it wasn't a big deal, I wouldn't be bringing it up.

When you stand in that position, the person in front of you notices. Their subconscious brain reads it and files the information that says you are not Alpha... the leader. You are most likely standing this way because you don't want to be or don't feel comfortable being the leader, even if you are saying something that seems to evoke leadership.

Maybe it's the years of trying to implement something you are excited about but you feel like no one else is on board. Maybe it's constantly dealing with the worry that you are hurting someone's feelings when you rightfully discipline. Maybe you are not in the best relationship with your wife at home and are worried about upsetting yet another woman in your life. Whatever it is, it is affecting your leadership.

A few months ago, I was on a call with a financial manager of a mid-sized office. She told me that her owner had offered her a promotion to the human resources manager position. However, as flattered as she was, she had to tell him that she could not take the position. The owner was surprised.

When he inquired as to why, she explained that he was the reason. She knew the girls in the office knew how to play him. Her concern was that if she had to hand out a disciplinary action to someone on the team, the girls knew that all they had to do to get their way was to start crying in front of the owner and he would give them what they wanted — thus undermining her responsibilities and her authority.

That is a classic example of an emasculated owner.

Maybe that is not you at all, or maybe you hope that is not you. I encourage you to look at areas in your office where you have become far more beta than you should be. A simple test is to look at how often you feel your ideas, suggestions or trainings are either overlooked or don't last, only to be replaced with someone else's better idea. It's your business, and it's your responsibility to make sure you are running it the best way it can be run.

In summary, successful operation of your business will only happen when everyone in the business is working from their **Why**, they understand the systems that are in place, and they are clear on their responsibilities. When you have these three things working together, your operation or business will not only be successful, but will also be something that other practitioners in your space envy.

Chapter Takeaway:

- Your practice is like a marriage. By learning to balance the Alpha and Beta in your practice, relationship management becomes much easier as you step into your role as a respected leader.

PART THREE

Relationships

RELATIONSHIPS

"Business is a cobweb of human relationships."

— *Ross Perot*

I believe the key to your success in *any* aspect of your life is found in the strength of your relationships. There is nothing in this life that you have not received or cannot receive successfully without your relationships.

We may be halfway through the CORE process, but I firmly believe a simple, guaranteed formula for amazing success can easily be found by building and strengthening your relationships, more than any other aspect of your business (assuming you have a basic knowledge of your profession).

When it comes to building relationships in business, most "experts" talk about them as a way to increase your referrals. From networking groups to "lunch and learns," surprise gifts and other swag, the common best practices to increase your relationships tend to be more akin to a desperate move than a genuine effort. I'm familiar with a few companies with committees whose purpose is to figure out new and innovative ways to "schmooze" other local businesses to refer business to them, rather than the competition.

What if that wasn't necessary? What if referrals were a natural occurrence because people *wanted* to be associated with who you are and what you represent, not because you gave them a bigger fruit bouquet at Christmas?

One orthodontist confided his utter disgust that there was an assumed "kiss-up" to all the local area's dentists to earn referrals. (He then revealed that he actually gets less than 10% of his business from them.)

In this section, I will not give you a single strategy to get more referrals with better networking ideas. I'm going to show you that the best marketing resource for new referrals won't cost you any of your money or your dignity.

I am not saying that it's not a good idea to have a presence within local networking groups or to be a member of the local chamber. But the days of feeling like you are "singing for your supper" will finally come to an end.

We are going to focus on the three relationships that I believe will have the greatest impact on your business.

1. The relationship with **yourself** (and your marriage)
2. The relationship with your **team**
3. The relationship with your **clients**

In that order. And yes, that is the hierarchy I believe you need to focus on in order to create the successful business you desire.

Combine these three areas with a specific culture and the referrals will come as an automatic result, not a desperate plea.

I know this firsthand. I have built a very successful business out of the thoughts in my head, first with the Business of Marriage, and second with the CORE, and I have done it all through focusing on the relationships around me. You can do the same. It all starts with the one area most private practice owners neglect — the relationship with yourself.

PERSONAL

* *

"The most important relationship you have in this life is the one you have with yourself. And then after that, I'd say once you have that, it may be hard work, but you can actually design your life."

— *Diane von Furstenberg*

A while back, after a speech I gave, a dentist (I'll call him Ted) introduced himself and thanked me for my training. I spoke on the topic of marriage and that the way you approach your marriage affects the way you approach your business.

In the training I reveal a map I created showing the seven steps to the death of a marriage. Ted explained that although he had been divorced for many years, he could completely relate and see where his marriage had followed the map. He was now going through his second divorce and asked if he could set up a time to talk to me after the event about his business. We exchanged information and the next week we were on a call.

We spent most of the time on the phone talking about Ted's personal feeling of self-worth, as well as his frustration that his marriage was ending in an ugly way, his relationship with his team was struggling, and between lawyer fees and other expenses on top of his dental practice bills, he was barely making it.

He used words like "failure," "stupid," "embarrassed" and "idiot" to describe himself and the situation he was in. He was upset that an educated person such as himself couldn't figure out how to run a business, be a real leader to his team and have the life he really wanted. His self-worth was at an all-time low.

Although he could not invest in my mentoring program, I decided to connect with him for the next few months just hoping to bring some encouragement and help where I could. The calls became less and less frequent, and he asked me to follow up with him towards the end of the year.

It was about six months later, through a mutual friend, that I heard Ted had taken his own life.

Of course my mind raced through all the things I wish I could have said or done to help more. I struggled with the guilt of not calling him the month prior when I thought of him, but got too busy. Could that have been the difference in his choosing another path?

I know I deal with a certain clientele whose stress level can be especially high. Studies have shown that dentists, in particular, show higher rates of drug use and suicide — some of the highest in the country. I am fully aware of the possibilities of tragedy. Yet it still hits hard.

I will never know what made Ted feel like there was no other choice. What I can tell you, if you are reading this, and you are struggling, is that you are not alone. There is another choice. The saying is true. This too will pass.

As I explained at the beginning of this book, as a professional entrepreneur, no one ever taught you how to deal with the business side of your profession. They certainly did not teach you about the emotional toll involved and how to take care of yourself mentally and emotionally.

You give to your clients, your team members, your business, your family, your friends, your church, your community; you give to everyone *long* before you give to yourself. Although the basic idea of that mindset is a good thing, it can often become a detriment to you and all those you are trying to serve. The phrase,

In order to give your best, you have to become a better receiver.

"First do no harm" needs to be directed to medical practitioners themselves first so that they can be at their best for their patients.

You have to take the time to recharge. The saying *you cannot give from an empty cup* is also true. In order to give your best, you have to become a better receiver. This sounds so simple from the outside. I know how hard it is for so many business owners, who provide a service of healing or fixing people, to give and give until you have nothing left. That is when burn out sets in. You are literally empty emotionally, and you start to disconnect from others.

When I have people come up to me and tell me how burned out they are, how drained they feel, how exhausted they have become, I know it's rarely ever due to the profession they choose, it's due to the lack of understanding of self-care.

The challenges with fatigue, burn out and tiredness are just the obvious results. The peripheral effects become frustration with employees, un-happiness in your marriage, and in many cases, depression, anxiety and low self-worth.

If you are not running efficiently mentally, spiritually and physically then you can't give all the talents and the skill that you have to each and every one of your clients. You might fool yourself into believing that you are able to zone out those stresses and frustrations when you are in the moment with a client. However, those emotions are running below the surface and have an impact on your all-around service. You are literally performing a disservice to your clients when you don't put yourself first.

So how do you put yourself first? How do you perform at your highest? How do you become your best self?

1. Have a Higher Purpose (Vision)

We have already talked about one of the key methods — having a clear vision and living in it everyday. That vision is your higher purpose in life and, when flushed out and used as the main driver for what you want to accomplish, and can act as a grounding source when things are becoming stressful.

Positive psychology tells us that the longest-lasting happiness in life and in business comes not from pleasure or profit, not even from passion (being in the zone or the flow of things), but from having a higher purpose. That is why your vision is the first thing we tackle in the book. It's also what most people lack.

Having a purpose that you are excited about will automatically increase your feeling of self-worth. When you walk into work every day with a focus and excitement about what you do and who you do it for, words like "failure," "loser" or "stupid" don't even come to mind. When you have a challenge, it doesn't hold you back or stop you; instead, your brain goes into "How do I overcome this?" mode.

Let me give you an example:

When it comes to your own feeling of self-worth, think of where you are on a scale of 1 to 10. If your self-talk consists of phrases like, "I'm not good enough," "I should be able to figure this out,"

"I'm a loser," "I can't believe this is so hard," and other previously mentioned words, your sense of self-worth will be represented by a lower number; "10" indicates that you know you are an amazing person, with great skill and talent, people admire you, your life is awesome, you have it all dialed in, and you have all the energy, self-belief and "I can do this" attitude you need.

Pick a number representing where you land.

Self-Worth: 1   2   3   4   5   6   7   8   9   10

Next, think of a challenge you are currently facing in your business and place it on another scale of 1-10, with "1" barely registering as a challenge and "10" representing a mountain of a challenge — one that has the possibility of closing your business down. (I'm not going to give you an example because what might be a huge challenge for you might not be to someone else reading the book.)

Pick a number representing the severity of the challenge as you see it.

Challenge: 1   2   3   4   5   6   7   8   9   10

If your self-image number is lower than your challenge number, know that there is only one number you actually have control of — the number tied to your personal self-image.

If you are living with a belief system that you are at a "4", then anything above that number on the challenge scale is going to look like a huge problem; a level "7" problem to a level "4" self-image is enough to stop you from moving forward.

The fact is, the "challenge," whatever it is, will not change. The only thing that can change is you. You don't even have to become a level "10" person for the level "7" challenge to no longer hold you back. An "8" will do.

Living with a true purpose is, in my humble opinion, the fastest and most rewarding way to increase your own self-value. When you are living a purpose-based, vision-focused life, things that were once big challenges become minor issues. Living in that higher purpose automatically makes you become bigger than your challenge.

2. Take Time for You

Make sure that you take time for yourself, schedule time to do whatever you enjoy, whatever fills your soul, whatever it is that makes you happy.

What (besides work) causes you to lose sense of time? Do you have a hobby, a fun sport, or a certain favorite place that you visit? Find a way to connect with them, every month, at a *minimum*, but preferably every week.

You must schedule time to rejuvenate. The key word is *schedule*. If you don't actually schedule it, the chances of it happening are slim to none.

If it is hard for you to think of actually taking time because of some misguided sense of sacrifice or a "workaholic" syndrome, then think of it as a service for your business, to make you the best at what you do, and more able to serve your clients better.

When you take time for yourself to do something outside of your everyday work, you will open yourself up to more creative solutions. If you look at the most successful people in the country or the world, they tend to be the most creative as well.

In a program I teach called Purpose & Passion, I encourage people who are stuck creatively in their business to take part in dance classes, piano or guitar, art classes, pottery class, woodworking, or start writing that book, learn a new language, or anything else that requires them to tap into their creative muscle. I believe that the only way you can get more creative is by being creative. If you become more creative on a personal level, that's automatically going to translate over into the business level. Creativity is an escape.

Another way to tap into that creativity, or escape day-to-day stress, is to make sure you have pleasant images in your business either in the public area, in your private office or both that are always visible. I have often recommended to my clients that they keep things in the office that remind them of their "happy place." Ten minutes in your office with the door shut surrounded by photos of your favorite golf destination, or movie posters, vacation spots — whatever relaxes you — will add much-needed stress relief to your day.

3. Make What You Say is a Priority a Priority

Because I started my business helping people have awesome marriages, it would be silly for me to not mention the power of your marriage and how it reflects in your business.

If you've missed the message that I have worked to drill into your head throughout this book, here it is again: *your relationships are everything*. I cannot stress enough how your marriage, in particular, directly impacts your performance in life, let alone in your business. I will shout it from the rooftops for the rest of my life. When your marriage is running at its best, you will feel more relaxed, more focused, more excited, and you'll be better able to overcome stressful situations.

You just have to decide to actually make it a priority, not just say it is a priority.

I write this next part knowing it might be a hard pill to swallow for many people, and I might even lose a few of you. It's important to know that I write it from a place of real caring and wanting the best for you. I do not apologize for saying it, because I have seen it over and over again, *and I am also guilty of it*.

I was talking to a new chiropractor client recently. He and his wife were talking about some of their marital issues, and one of the biggest challenges she had with him was that he'd come home exhausted every day.

He gets up at 5:00 in the morning, gets ready and goes to work, spends all day in the office and sees over 100 people in a day. His wife informed me that he would come home spent to the point that he would immediately sit down on the couch and zone out with the TV, a cycle that repeated each day.

On the weekends, he would spend a majority of his time on his cell phone or computer answering emails. When out at the kids' activities or even on a supposed date, he would either be distracted by his phone or talking about work. Their last "getaway" was to a chiropractic convention where she spent most of her time alone, with the other wives there, or she sat at the same table at an event just to feel like she spent time with him.

They did have one non-work vacation, but he spent so much of his time stressed about the happenings at the office that it took most of the fun out of it. Her biggest complaint was, "We have no time together... I don't feel like our family, or me, are a priority."

She was right, and he knew it.

If I were to ask most people reading this book, "What is the most important thing in the world to you?" They would most likely reply with "family" or something similar.

Here is the hard truth. If you relate to my example above (or if your spouse does), then your declaration of what is "most important" to you is obviously not true. Don't get me wrong — that doesn't mean you don't care for them, love them and want the best for them. It just simply means they are not the most important to you. In life, we give the most focus to the thing that is the most important in our minds.

I am not saying that you don't have to give attention to your business or that you should not be focused on your clients. However, if your wife and family are telling you they feel like they come second in your life, do yourself a favor and take that as a hint.

Right now, some of you might be thinking of a few choice words for me with the various justifications like, "I am doing this for my family" or "I would like to do more to focus on them, but (insert your reasons here)."

The fact is, for everything in life, we either have reasons or results. If your results are an unhappy marriage, a disconnected family unit and overwhelming stress and frustration, then it's time to stop the reasons and get new results.

The number one rule I always start any trainings with is that you are responsible for you. It is a basic truth that is meant to stop people from blaming something or someone else for their results. I hope you see that my intention for this book is to help you get the results you really want.

> For everything in life, we either have reasons or results.

4. Live Like a Rock Star!

When it comes to taking more off your plate, releasing stress and feeling like you are the master of your own time, this one tip will change your world. The problem is that most people take much more convincing than they should to actually do it. Get a personal assistant.

In the Responsibilities section, we discussed delegation in your business. Having a personal assistant allows for delegation in your life.

There is a reason rock stars and Hollywood-types have personal assistants to take care of the everyday minutia that they don't have the brain space or time to take on. They understand their time is worth more than the assistant costs. And a good assistant will be able to handle things faster and better than they would.

From answering emails, screening calls, picking up lunch, dropping off the dry cleaning, buying gifts for loved ones and all-around taking care of their daily schedule, the assistant is not a luxury, he or she is a necessity if you are serious about getting your time back.

You are important in the lives of the people you help. You are a rock star, so start treating yourself like one.

I had to learn this lesson the hard way. It took me years of thinking about getting an assistant (and my wife telling me to get one) before I finally did it. I can honestly tell you that it is the reason why my business has taken off over the last few years. From arranging discovery sessions with potential clients, scheduling my mentoring calls with current clients, creating presentations for my webinars, doing simple graphic design, coordinating with my web people, contacting new offices, following up with speaking engagements, picking up my kids from school when needed, dropping me off at the airport, to even reviewing and editing this book, my assistant does so many things. And I used to think I had to do it all.

That is my list. What would your list be? Take a second and list some of the things that you would love to have someone do for you.

What a personal assistant could take off my shoulders:

_____

_____

_____

_____

_____

_____

_____

_____

_____

_____

_____

_____

_____

One of my concerns was whether I would actually have enough for my assistant to do in order to justify the cost. If you are thinking the same thing, you can always start the person off on a part-time basis and see how it works. That is what I ended up doing, and within a month I had given her full time status.

Try it out for three months and see how it changes your life (or not).

If you want more time, more creativity, more focus, more peace of mind, more stress relief, less frustration, do not pass GO — hire an assistant as soon as possible.

Not sure where to get started in looking for an assistant?

First, ask your current team members if they know of anyone who might be looking. Then, widen the search out to your friends and family members.

Next, go to craigslist.com and place a simple ad. For a template to find your rock star assistant, sign up for *The Path to the Propreneur* at thepracticecure.com.

5. Get More Sleep

I know it sounds obvious and for some of you easier said than done, but the science is in and it's stacking up more and more every year. Lack of sleep is one of the major causes of stress in life. You cannot perform at your best if you are not getting the correct amount of sleep.

A moment ago I talked about the benefits of taking ten minutes in your office with the door shut. Ten minutes of meditation a day will do you wonders. Companies like Google and the Huffington Post have nap rooms for their employees because they understand the power of being at your best (and the detriment of working tired all day).

In her book *Thrive*, Arianna Huffington explains that taking a daily nap was just one of the many lifestyle choices she had to make after waking up in a pool of her own blood after she had collapsed exhausted on the floor of her study and had cut open her head as she fell.

She had gotten to a place of so much overwork, stress, burn out and fatigue that one night her body simply gave out on her. She then decided to study how to better mentally take care of her mind and body, and allowance for naptime came to be.

If you get anything from this section, I hope it is that you are the most important aspect of your business. The best investment you can make in your business is in yourself and your health.

For some of you that are used to just putting your head down and moving forward with no regard to your true needs and dismiss the importance of the previous recommendations, I hope you reconsider. Take a nap? Take a dance class? Hire an assistant? It just doesn't fit into your schedule. Your situation is different, right?

Wrong!

Maybe you are not yet at the place of collapsing in your home like Arianna, but how close are you? Do you really want or need for something that dramatic to cause you to make a change in your life? Do yourself, your family and your business a favor and consider Arianna's and Ted's stories your wake up call.

What if I'm right? What if these few simple suggestions were the answer you have been looking for? What if the burn out, the frustration and the stress could actually be a thing of the past? Here's a serious yet obvious question, how has what you have been trying been working out for you? Is your best idea to just keep pushing through, doing the same thing you have been doing, figuring that this is just the way it is or just hoping that things will eventually magically get better?

I challenge you to implement just-for-you time for just three months. If you're overwhelmed by shifting all at once, take just one of the suggestions and commit to it for 90 days and see if you notice a difference in your life. See if your cup feels any more full.

Chapter Takeaway:

- You cannot give from an empty cup. In order to be at your best, you have to learn to be a better receiver.

- Perform at your best by living for your higher purpose, taking personal time, sorting out your priorities, hiring an assistant and getting better sleep.

TEAM

"Believing the customer is always right is a subconscious way of favoring the customer over the employee, which can lead to resentment among employees. When managers put the employees first, the employees will then put the customers first. Put employees first and they will be happy at work."

— *Alexander Kjerulf, Happy Hour is 9 to 5*

The best business minds agree. Your employees care more about your business if they know you care about them. However, there is an interesting dynamic between you and your team. On one hand, you are the boss and need to keep a certain level of professionalism. On the other hand, your employees feel more connected to you when you show a genuine interest in them and their lives outside the office.

One doctor stated that if he had to spend energy to think about an employee's life or problems after he had gone home, then that employee was not a good fit for his office. Another doctor felt that the members of his office should just be happy to have a job. Yet another doctor made sure to take at least one big trip with the entire office team every year. Another client of mine makes it a priority to know as much detail as he can about the employees' lives, even going so far as to making sure he is aware of team members' family birthdays so that he can send a gift.

I believe a good balance can be found.

If you have followed along and implemented what I have explained so far, you are already on the path to building stronger relationships with your team. When you found out your team members *Why*, you discovered a new way of engaging them in their current positions and how to utilize their skills and talents in a new way. Finding out what their "support style" is helped you crack the code of encouragement and appreciation in order to get more out of them.

Your employees care more about the business if they know you care about them.

Most of all, when you created specific core values, you gave them a clear outline of what was expected of them and how they can help you reach your goals. These simple, valuable systems and processes have already set you on the path to making your team members a priority.

Now, we are going to dig even **deeper** to help you create a team other practices will envy!

What would it mean to you if you had an active part in creating new protocols, workflow and the new hire process? Would you feel like you are a contributor to the success of the office, rather than a worker drone?

Would you feel more included if your employer had a monthly "State of the Practice" meeting where they disclosed the financial successes as well as challenges the office is having?

These are just a few ways you can easily strengthen your relationship with your **team**! And *there* is your first lesson.

Team vs. Staff

Throughout this book, I hope you have noticed that I don't like to use the word "staff" when referring to the people who work with you. I eluded to this earlier. It's a bit of a pet peeve of mine. Your choice of word matters.

A "staff" is an infection that nobody wants. Successful companies don't focus on building a staff. They instead create a team.

The popular business model of new professional graduates buying existing practices means most owners don't get to focus on building a team of their own, they inherit one. Most spend a few years as an associate buying out the practice and get used to "how things are done." By the time they get to take over full ownership, the habits of the employees are set and accepted as normal. Even if they would like to change things up, the focus of building a team of their own is usually not a priority when there are so many other seemingly more important business needs to be met.

Sally is a dentist who took over her father's practice. Her father trained her in how to take care of clients, not how to grow a practice. When she took over, she figured she would keep doing what her dad did and things would work out. After all, it seemed to work for him. However, because Sally did not focus on her vision, her core values, and creating the team she wanted, fifteen years later, she had an unmotivated team who treated their jobs as if they had tenure, along with a rapidly declining clientele.

How could Dr. Sally turn this staff into a team that could help her turn the business around? The most basic thing I could think of was to have the doctor come clean.

I instructed her to call a company meeting and explain all the challenges the business was facing, then to simply ask for everyone's help. Find out who would be willing to help turn the business around.

Dr. Sally was nervous. She called me the day before and I helped her lay out a "come to Jesus" speech that laid out the situation and then asked each one of the employees to come to her individually and tell her if they were in or not. Emotionally, this was a huge leap for the doctor.

The result? A team was born. Every member told her they were in, no matter what it took. They assured her that they believed in her and knew they could turn things around.

As of this writing, it has only been a few weeks, and already the office has a renewed atmosphere. Old habits are being broken and attitudes are positive. Now that she has a team, I know they will achieve their goals.

Hire the Right People

Instead of buying into an existing practice, some new and daring professionals choose to start a practice from scratch. In the hiring process, they typically focus on getting people in the needed job positions so they can open the doors and start accepting clients. The immediate need of filling a position with a person technically qualified to do the job becomes greater than the long-term focus of hiring the right people to fulfill your vision.

Some owners even know in their gut that this person is not going to work out, but due to the pressure of opening the doors, decide to hope for the best. However, "hope" is never a good business plan for building a powerful team. A few years later, you are dealing with an employee who is the cause of many headaches and complaints; yet, it's too much of a pain for you to have to let them go and deal with hiring someone new.

Diana had worked in Dr. Tim's office for over 15 years. She was his front desk attendant. Instead of being a powerful first impression and representation of the type of awesome care the client was about to receive from Dr. Tim, she was not engaging; she was unmotivated and even rude on multiple occasions. When he would share his disappointment with her and try to correct the behavior, she would either brush it off by saying he was being too sensitive, or if the behavior did change, it was only briefly.

When Dr. Tim told me of his frustration with Diana, I asked the same question you are probably asking yourself now: "Why would you have her in that position, or in your office at all for that matter?"

His response? "She has been with me from the beginning. Deep down, she is a good person."

When he learned the importance and freedom of creating a team that served his vision, and empowered them with core values, he realized things had to change. He offered her the opportunity to participate in his new focus in the practice. She fought it, and he ended up having to let her go.

Diana, the "good person" who he kept around for years, even though she was the epitome of **staff**, promptly sued him for wrongful termination.

I believe most people who work in the health care industry want to serve others. The majority of employees want to provide support to their owners. Most want to have a fun, exciting place where they are proud to work. If you have that type of team, then great for you! You have obviously done a lot of things right, either by design or by default.

Unfortunately, some of you have either inherited or unknowingly grown staff that have infected others in your office or, in some cases, taken over all together. When you have one staff member that is depressed, lonely, upset, jealous, causing drama or feeling slighted, it's going to affect the entire office.

How do you know if you have a staff infection? Here are just a few examples of possible symptoms:

- Decreased productivity
- Gossip, conflicts or hostility towards one another or you
- Confusion about assignments
- Lack of goals or consistently unaccomplished goals
- Assignments not carried through properly
- Apathy toward new processes or requests
- Lack of involvement
- Bringing personal drama into the workplace
- Lack of initiation, imagination, innovation
- Unwilling to problem solve for themselves
- Complaints of discrimination or favoritism
- Ineffective or low participation in team meetings
- Negative reactions to the manager's requests
- Sabotaging of new policies
- Complaints about quality of service

I could go on, but I think you get the idea. Some of you may easily identify a few people in the office who fit these descriptions.

So, what do you do?

If you are serious about creating the practice you want, you have two choices.

Enroll them into your new vision and give them the opportunity to opt in, or, you'll have to support their decision to opt out by letting them go.

Fear is a terrible way to run a business.

I know that is not always easy. In some cases, there is fear of negative repercussions (i.e. Dr. Tom's situation) that can paralyze you and keep you from moving forward with what you know needs to be done. So do it correctly. I am not an attorney. Go talk to yours and ask about the proper way to end employment in your state.

For the majority of you, it's not that dramatic. You have to step up and find the courage to design a practice you want, even with the potential of hard feelings. Fear is a terrible way to run a business.

Leading marketing and business consultant Lisa Marie Wark bluntly explains the challenge before you, as well as some steps to make it happen:

> *"Rarely does a business, especially a small one, have the luxury of cleaning house... Instead, most bosses are faced with a level of corporate dysfunction that is composed of a workplace of long time colleagues, friends, or perhaps family members who have developed bad attitudes, bad habits, and a bad product. It's not easy to tell any of these folks that they suck, especially after you have enabled them in their particular less than stellar performance for a protracted amount of time."*

That last part might be difficult to absorb. The hard fact is, when it comes to your team — if the relationships in your office are not in alignment, if you have more staff members than team members, that is not a "them" problem, it's a leadership problem. You have to be a different kind of leader.

How do you do that?

1. Decide to make a change.

Keep moving forward *even when* it's hard.

Leaders feel the fear and do what is right for the business anyway. You should expect a moderate to significant amount of pushback at the beginning. It will come from those who do not want to give up the stronghold of influence they have had until now. They have shaped the culture the way they are comfortable with, regardless of what you want.

Even when you are disappointing some people, you have to be dedicated to your vision and values and move forward.

2. Lead by example.

You have to take the leadership position. You cannot delegate this out to anyone else. Share your new vision with them and then live that vision. If you have a core value to "Only have good days and great days" then you have to live up to that, even when you don't feel like it.

3. Spell it out for them.

Better yet, have them spell it out for *you* so that you know they are on the same level of understanding. Do not leave room for individual interpretation. Make sure you are clear and specific on *any* matter you think might not be clear. Ask them for their understanding of what they think is being asked of them.

After starting the CORE program, Dr. Abramowitz wanted to make sure everyone was in total understanding of his vision and the company's core values. He had every team member fill out a worksheet with their understanding of what each core value and the vision meant to them. When he got the worksheets back, the majority of them were in alignment with what he expected. A few were not. This gave him the opportunity to have an individual meeting with those members and clarify what he was looking for and get everyone on the same page.

Creating the team you want may seem like a battle when you are in the middle of it, but it's a battle you can win through patience and determination. If you exercise those traits, you will no doubt find your employees exercising them as well.

Team Relationship Builders

Now that you have the team you want, how do you continually and purposefully strengthen those relationships?

1. Make your team the most important client you have.

Offer your services to your team member and their immediate family members at no charge. Give them your best service. Make them a priority. How much better will someone be at touting your services when they have personally gained from them?

I have seen offices that do not spend a dime on marketing because the team is the best marketing they can buy. The team has become not only the best resource for referrals, because they have firsthand knowledge of the quality of service, they are able to be a source of integrity when promoting those services.

2. Pay a fair wage, but compensate more than they expect.

If you pay average, you will get an average performance. Show them that you are willing to compensate for a job above and beyond by hitting goals, showing initiative and going the extra mile.

Be smart about it. Don't just give raises based upon longevity of employment. I spoke with an orthodontist whose TC was making close to $35 an hour because she had worked there for so long, but her closing ratio was at about 50%. The doctor was concerned about the sluggish production rate of her office. I pointed out that the TC had no incentive to be better at sales because her income was not connected to her close rate. Even though the office was struggling, she was still getting her $35 an hour.

Dan Sullivan once said at an event, "Your payroll should be your highest expense in your business." I agree.

3. Quarterly Retreats

In the Operations chapter, I wrote about the importance of daily team meetings. To really help build the relationship with your team, consider quarterly retreats — they provide an amazing ROI.

When a team can get together outside of the office to learn, plan, play and relax, they build a stronger bond with one another. That bond will deliver more creativity in solving problems and develop a sense of unity once they get back to the office.

For all your meetings, make sure you take time to plan them. Have specific goals in mind for the meetings. Include trainings, discussions and masterminds on how the business can improve. You can have fun as well as achieve goals.

4. State of the Company Address

In 2014, social media sharing company Buffer did a rather unorthodox thing: they revealed their pay structure (right down to the CEO's salary) in a blog post. The company was then inundated with resumes.

While on a call one day with a practice owner and discussing struggling finances, she said, "I know they (her team) all think I have more money than God."

I inquired, "Why don't you tell them where you are? They might surprise you with some ideas on how they can help."

Her reply was not one that surprised me. "I don't think that is any of their business."

I beg to differ. It's their jobs and livelihood too.

Being transparent with your team has many relationship-building qualities. Many larger companies are seeing the benefit of this with their employees.

I am not suggesting you post your monthly sales numbers on your social media. What I am suggesting is sharing your numbers and the "state of the company" with your employees regularly.

Instead of making them feel like they are just along for the ride, choosing to operate a transparent business with your team demonstrates that you have respect for them. It also gives them a feeling of team involvement. Team members who don't know what's going on in your business may speculate, participate in spreading gossip, or be unsure and anxious about the state of the company and the security of their jobs. Lastly, it's a great way to build team loyalty. When you have open and honest communication with members of your team, employees are much more likely to have a higher degree of morale and job satisfaction.

5. Give Goals and Deadlines

We already covered the importance of having specific expectations and responsibilities. One of the strongest ways you can cultivate a stronger relationship with your team is by giving them the chance to work together accomplishing goals.

In January of 2015, Dr. Datwyler challenged his team to a goal of hitting 40 new orthodontic patients in one month. What's their usual average? 30. The bond for the team grew stronger with every new patient they were able to tally up on the handmade goal chart. They had to make a few changes, work together through a few challenges, and were able to see where some of their systems were a bit weaker than they thought. In the end not only did they hit their goal, but they were a better team for it.

Without continuous and specific goals you lose out on the chance to see performance gaps, growth gaps, opportunity gaps and training gaps.

What's in a Name?

I started this section with the importance of the word you use to describe the people who work for you. I want to end this section with a similar focus — the words you use to describe the different functions of the office.

By being creative with the titles in your office, you make your team members feel unique and special. The unique title can also serve as marketing to your clients. Sending a potential new client to the "Client Care Coordinator" or "Director of First Impressions" sounds a whole lot better to a client than The Scheduler. I'm sure you can see how it would make the team member feel special as well.

A unique title like Client Concierge adds an immediate image and value far beyond "the front desk girl."

The Treatment Plan Guide	Patient Advocate
Treatment Advocate	Finance Wizard
Smile Director	Smile Architect
Miracle Workers	Quality Controllers
Secretary of Defense	Ambassador of Buzz
Chief Cheerleader	Chief Amazement Officer

There is power in a name.

Take a moment and think of a few of the positions in your office that can use a name upgrade.

Write down a few of them here:

_____

_____

_____

_____

_____

Creativity with simple things like titles for positions and rooms is just one more way to set you apart, make you memorable and build unique relationships.

Good relationship-building skills will help you unite your employees around a common goal and generate greater productivity. Without this as a focus, you will limit the growth of the company and create a work environment that suffers.

Building relationships with your team is an ongoing process. It will help your practice evolve into a cohesive unit. The team members not only share expectations for accomplishing group tasks, but trust and support one another and respect one another's individual differences. Your role as a leader is to guide your team toward cohesiveness and productivity. A team takes on a life of its own and you have to regularly nurture and maintain it, just as you would any relationship you care about.

> Good relationship-building skills will unite your employees around a common goal and generate greater productivity.

BONUS

Let's call this Finding the needle in a haystack, made easy.

One of the biggest challenges many practices have is finding the right people to work for them. Mostly due to the fact that most people don't know what they want in an employee or team member. Now that you understand you're the power of the CORE you are perfectly positioned to learn some powerful hiring methods.

Go to thepracticecure.com to learn the secret method to hiring the right people for your practice.

Chapter Takeaway:

- Your employees care more about your business if they know you care about them.

- Eliminate "staff infections" by hiring the right people from the start. Confront any "staff" members and invite them to become part of the team.

- Use team relationship builders to create more unity and strengthen inner-office relationships.

CLIENTS

"We see our customers as invited guests to a party, and we are the hosts. It's our job to make the customer experience a little bit better."

— Jeff Bezos, Amazon

Although the relationship with your clients is placed last in this section, please do not mistake that for lack of importance. Of course, without clients continually walking through your doors, you have no business.

You have most likely heard the phrase "People do business with people they know, like, and trust." True as that might be, in the professional healthcare industry, most people do business with you, minus the "know" part.

How much do your clients really know you? I would venture to bet that if we took a survey of your clients and asked them a series of personal questions about you, the majority would get less than 30% right. They might know how many kids you have because of the huge picture you have on the wall. They might even know if you like baseball over football due to a random conversation you once had. Yet when it comes to really knowing you, most of your clients do business with you based upon the "like" and "trust" factor more than the "know."

That's not a bad thing! Two out of the three is a pretty good average. What if we could make that a three out of three? How much would that increase the relationship level with your clients? The stronger a relationship is with you, the greater the loyalty to you and the more likely that clients will be advocates, nay evangelicals for your business.

Studies show time and again that loyal customers are the most apt to tell their friends about your business. This creates a very strong word-of-mouth form of marketing. Word-of-mouth marketing is the most important element of any marketing campaign.

Your relationship-building responsibility doesn't just fall on your shoulders. This is a team effort relying on the "before-during-after" and other systems in the previous sections.

Now, it's time to build upon those relationships by showing each of your clients how important they are to you.

Tell Them Your Story

Throughout this book I have tried to share as many stories with you as possible. I have shared some important details of personal clients, as well as illustrated big picture examples from the world of business. Stories connect people together. They allow for a sense of common understanding, even if someone did not go through the exact same experience as someone else.

From the stage, knowing that not everyone in the audience has gone through a divorce as a child, I will ask, "Have you ever felt like you had no control or say in a situation in your life?" Everyone can relate to not being in control at one point in their life, even if they can't completely relate to being a child of divorce.

Connect with your "audience" by telling your story. *Not* your resume, your story. Why do you do what you do? What is it that made you take a risk, study for years and become the person who feels they can help others in your profession? Tell them your story and you will create an immediate connection.

Where do you do this? In our social media society, we have multiple outlets to do so, but let's start with one of the biggest (and most boring) mistakes I see on a weekly basis — your website.

I visit multiple professional websites a week. I want to keep up on the new and best practices in the industries I serve. Let me sound like my grandpa when I say, "If I had a quarter for every time I saw a *Meet the Doctor* page, and all it did was list a bland bio consisting of where he went to school and other credentials, I'd be rich." Give me another quarter for the professional picture of the doctor standing in a field somewhere and I'd already be retired.

How about actually letting the potential client meet you? This is a perfect area to tell your story. Show some pictures of you in action riding a motorbike, at your favorite sports game or playing with your kids. This is how you make a connection. This is how you get people to know who you are.

I am not saying the picture and resume with degrees and associations is a bad thing, it just shouldn't be the only thing. Also remember that your story is a continual adventure.

Utilize resources like blog posts, newsletters, both online and offline, Facebook, Twitter, Instagram, and other social media to share your story, announce accomplishments and spread case studies.

BONUS

Want to really set yourself apart?

Publish a book. Having a book published gives you automatic credibility as well as a huge impressiveness factor. Imagine your book sitting on the counter when your new patient walks in. Better yet, imagine handing a signed copy to every new or potential patient. Talk about your expert positioning and relationship building.

It's not as hard as you think. It's definitely not as expensive as you would think. It can be about $50-$100 for your first round, and you can have it done within a week. Answer the questions on the following pages as thoroughly as possible, review the steps that follow, then sign up for The Path to the Propreneur at thepracticecure.com.

Step 1: Answer the following questions in paragraph form:

Why did you get into this profession? What drove you to it? Is there a connection as a child? Did any experience stand out that influenced your decision?

_____

_____

_____

_____

_____

_____

_____

_____

Where did you go to school? What was your experience there?

_____

_____

_____

_____

_____

_____

_____

_____

When did you first know that you wanted to be a(n) _____?

_____

_____

_____

_____

_____

_____

_____

_____

What was your biggest challenge in getting there?

_____

_____

_____

_____

_____

_____

_____

_____

What drives you every day?

_____

_____

_____

_____

_____

_____

_____

_____

What gives you the most joy?

_____

_____

_____

_____

_____

_____

_____

What have you learned about balance?

_____

_____

_____

_____

_____

_____

_____

What's the best lesson you have learned about being a(n) _____?

_____

_____

_____

_____

_____

_____

_____

What is your vision for your patients/clients?

_____

_____

_____

_____

_____

_____

_____

One of your favorite success stories:

_____

_____

_____

_____

_____

_____

_____

Step 2: Write out each of your core values and your vision. Below each one, give an explanation of what each means to you. Ask each member of your team to do the same. Tell them their answers will be public.

Step 3: Write a paragraph on what you feel the company culture is or what you hope it to be. Ask each member of your team to do the same. Tell them their answers will be public.

Step 4: When finished, either enlist someone in your office or hire out someone to transcribe your story and your answers into paragraph form, creating your first chapter. (Fiverr.com is a great resource where you can get this done professionally for about $5.)

Step 5: Format your core values vision and culture questions to create chapter 2.

Step 6: Format your team members' answers into the subsequent chapters.

Step 7: Find the "expert positioning report" I instructed you to create earlier, then add that as the second half of the book.

Step 8: Write a simple wrap-up and thank you for the final chapter.

Step 9: Have your book formatted for Amazon's self-publishing platform CreateSpace at www.createspace.com and have a book cover designed using the specs from CreateSpace using fiverr.com.

Step 10: Order a sample of your book. Then buy 20 copies for your first round.

Depending on the size of your office as well as the size of your report, you should have a page count of about 30-75 pages.

You are now a published author. No, it's not going to be a New York Times bestselling title, but it doesn't need to be. You've just built a "wow" factor that separates you from the others in your field.

Like and Trust

Let's look into how you can increase your "Like and Trust" relationship factor with your clients through your customer service.

From 1997-2001, I had the privilege of working for Nordstrom. In customer service lore, there are few stories that demonstrate the essence of customer service more than the legendary Nordstrom tire story. The story goes that a man went to a Nordstrom store to return a set of tires. Nordstrom, a high-end clothing and shoe store, doesn't sell tires. The customer asserted that he had purchased the tires there, and the salesperson accepted the tires and refunded the customer the amount paid for the tires. Let me repeat... the salesperson refunded the customer the price of a set of tires... at a clothes store!

This story sounds like an exaggeration, though when I went through my Nordstrom University customer service training, they still told it. Exaggerated or not, this story has been repeated often enough to become part of Nordstrom lore. It inspires the employees of Nordstrom Corporation to strive for those levels of customer service that can become legendary stories.

You see, customer service is not only the level of customer care and attention you provide. It is your reputation for customer service. It's that reputation that makes people like and trust Nordstrom as a department store leader.

When it comes to creating that type of likeability and trustworthiness, focus on these key areas:

1. Value Their Time

Recall the story of my doctor client who took a day off to see an orthodontist, only to be told he'd have to take an additional day or two off before actually getting the braces on. For the orthodontist in this situation, not respecting the patient's time cost him more than just that one case. If my client is talking to me about it, you know he's told others. That is not a great way to build a relationship of trust.

Show your potential clients that you value their time by making sure the appointment coordinator explains exactly what to expect as the appointment is being booked. Don't just give them a time frame; give them an outline of what is going to happen at the appointment. Is it possible to get treatment started right away? If not, what are the options?

This process of explanation should happen throughout the entire patient experience, not just on the first call or even just the first visit, for that matter. In this case had the patient known he could not get the treatment started on the same day, he would have never come in and lost out on the day in his office. Don't assume your patient knows what to expect. For you, it's what you deal with every day, for them, it's a new experience entirely. All of these explanations will make them feel like they are part of the process and that you want to honor the time they are spending with you.

2. Show Enthusiasm

I had braces for five years as a teenager. (Ironically, I was a terrible patient!) I have spent my fair share of time sitting in a waiting room, waiting for my name to be called. Let's face it, that room for a kid can have a sense of heightened anticipation. I still remember taking my seat with the other unenthused people, waiting until the assistant came with a file in hand to the door or the opening that led to the back of the office. It seemed everyone would look up from their *National Geographic* or *People* magazine in unison to see if their name was to be called next.

When my name would finally be called, it was done one of two ways — as a question (as if the assistant is questioning if patients are showing up) or monotone (Bueller... Bueller...). Very rarely was it with a tone of enthusiasm to see me, or out of familiarity. Never did they come any further into the waiting room than the threshold leading back to the dental chairs.

To this day, whenever I go to the doctor or dentist and I am waiting to be beckoned to the back, I am reminded of all those times as a little boy waiting my turn. I'll admit that maybe there is a bit less of the impending doom feeling and a little more of a welcoming tone from the assistant, but you know what hasn't changed? The inability of the assistant to pass beyond the threshold and venture into the waiting room to greet me.

During my initial observation period for body language training, this is one of the areas I look for. If an assistant is willing to pass beyond the threshold and go get the patient in order to lead them back, or if she implements the call-and-wait strategy. Unfortunately, almost every time it's the latter.

Your clients want to know that you care they are there. They want to be personally greeted with enthusiasm, not beckoned from a distance. Even if there's a routine, clients deserve to be treated specially every time.

It's not just in the way you greet them, either. It's in the complete experience they have while in your office.

Some simple suggestions you can do to show enthusiasm:

- Treat new clients like celebrities: Make them feel like they have just joined an exclusive club. Focus on amazing them beyond the service they were expecting. Ask yourself what would pleasantly "shock" you if you were the client? Do that.

- Greet each patient by venturing into the waiting area, call the patient by the right name, shake the person's hand, and lead him or her where you want him or her to go while giving at least one compliment. Never just call out a name and tell the patient to "head on back."

- When the patient's appointment is done, don't just send him on his way. Walk him to the front. This will allow you to be sure he books the next appointment, but it also makes the patient feel important.

- If you're an orthodontist and you have a client who has accepted treatment, celebrate it by bringing the client out to the floor and announcing it to the rest of the team. Depending on your culture, you could sing a song or shout a cheer of congratulations.

- As a team, celebrate important accomplishments the client has made in the progress of treatment. At the halfway mark of treatment, celebrate "hump day."

- Create a simple monthly newsletter that lets people know what is going on in your practice. Hit a certain goal? Announce it. New clients? Feature them. Happy clients? Show the before and after. Tough case? Celebrate the success. What about team members' and their kids' accomplishments? Brag about them. List birthdays, graduations, anniversaries, births... be creative. Part of building a culture is getting people excited about what you are up to and what is happening in their "club." A newsletter is a very simple way to do that.

- At the end of treatment, create a process that makes the person feel special. Again, depending on your culture, it could be a special celebration with the entire team or a special reward of accomplishment given privately.

Your turn! What are some ways that you can make your clients feel your enthusiasm towards them? Write down at least 3 ways.

_____

_____

_____

_____

3. Be Open and Honest

This might seem obvious, and I hope it's not needed, but sometimes we can be tempted to hold back bad news for fear of a reaction, even if it's not in your control. When we know the results will be disappointing or even hurtful to the client or the clients' parents, it's easy to want to soft-sell them the truth. After all, your job is to heal, not to hurt.

If the treatment you initially suggested is not working the way you had hoped, *let them know*. If you don't know why, don't make something up. Reaffirm that you are committed to finding out why, and go forward. If it's a mistake you made, admit it quickly with a plan to correct it.

If they are not participating in their treatment in the way you need them to, tell them sooner rather than later. When you are not completely open with them, it only hurts your reputation.

Remember what your mother taught you! Honesty is the best policy.

4. Be Personable

Again, this may seem obvious, but when you are having a bad day, are drained emotionally or feeling rushed, it's easy to forget that your "bedside manner" is an essential aspect of your client's treatment.

As mentioned, a successful relationship between you and your client requires mutual trust and respect. If the patient is uncomfortable with your demeanor or feels like she is just another warm body, how can the patient be expected to disclose private, sometimes embarrassing information?

It can also help legally. A 1994 study published by Vanderbilt University showed that doctors are more likely to be sued if patients feel the doctor was rude, rushed visits or failed to answer questions.

I'm pretty sure that no professional or team member sets out to be brusque or dismissive; however, the pressures of the day can cause reactions that may come off to clients as hurried or even rude. Maintaining a positive atmosphere is important in making patients feel comfortable and valued. This is especially true when patients may be apprehensive or even fearful of a visit to your office for treatment. It's much easier to build trust and develop a long-lasting relationship when there's a good connection made with a client.

5. Teach Your Core Values

I highly recommend that you display your core values in an area where all of your clients can see them. This tells your clients what you are all about and will actually help enroll them to participate in achieving them.

Being transparent in what you stand for, and what everyone believes as a company will definitely create a feeling of like and trust. People know what they are getting from you and what they can expect from you.

"But what if one of your values mentions money or making a profit," you ask?

Display it. Your clients need to know that you are in business to make money and the more successful you are at that, the better your service can be for them.

6. Ask for Referrals.

Now that you are providing amazing service, shocking them by making them feel like celebrities, truly getting to know them, and teaching them the core values you hold most dear, it's time to develop your referral program. They know, like and trust you. It's the most ideal time to ask.

If you don't have a referral program, you are 100% more likely not to get referrals. People don't get as many referrals as they would like is that they don't ask for referrals. (I know those last statements sound like they came from the files of Captain Obvious, but they're true!)

The challenge most people have with asking for referrals is that they don't do it at the right time. So when is the right time? When your clients are in their most excited emotional state. Maybe they hit an important benchmark in their treatment or they are excited about a specific result. Whatever that time is in your experience with them, make sure you introduce the program and ask for the referral then. Then, make sure you remind them... continually.

If you have gotten into the habit of mentioning the program when they first start treatment, never to mention it again, just hoping they will remember, that is not a program. That is a wish. You have to take control of the program and make sure it is a continual reminder in your marketing.

I gave you some ideas in the systems area about the phone message people hear while on hold. The previously mentioned newsletter idea is another avenue that can be useful. Here are a few more Do's and Don'ts to look out for in your referral program.

- **Don't:** *Ask the wrong person.* Asking or reminding "little Johnny" while he is on his way out the door will, 99% of the time, ensure that he forgets about it by the time he gets to the car.

- **Don't:** *Give them a weak incentive.* Does a $25 gift card, a T-shirt, a water bottle or an entrance to raffle get you excited? You can do better than that. These people are advertising for you. In some cases they are giving you a potential client worth thousands of dollars. I see a lot of raffles for iPhones or iPods and those are nice, but all you are offering is the *chance* to win. Save the raffles for patients who show up on time consistently, wear your shirt to the appointment, and actively participate in the treatment plan.

- **Don't:** *Hide or minimize your program.* Your referral program should be a part of your business plan, not a desperate "go-to" when you are lacking clientele. If you end up having a problem with too many clients because of your referral program, (not a bad problem to have), it's a lot easier to turn it off than it is to try and jumpstart a dead program. If you or your team is concerned about feeling like they are bothering people, it's time for some specific training on the value you are offering to people when you ask for a referral.

- **Do:** *Ask or remind mom / dad in the context of what a great job they are doing with "little Johnny's" progress.* When a person is feeling proud or emotionally attached to you they have a higher likelihood of wanting to share the good news with others. They are more likely to take the time and think of whom they would want to refer.

- **Do:** *Make sure you reward them with something they want.* When they are giving you a client, be sure to make your incentive something they are excited about, that makes them feel special. Concert or amusement park tickets, weekend stays at a nice resort, a day at the spa, experiences, or free services are all great. You want to do anything that makes them stop and take notice. If you really want to separate yourself from your competitors, stand out in the way you reward your clients for spreading the word. Depending on your ideal client, you need to make sure you have an incentive for what they actually want. If parents are the decision makers regarding your service, then make sure it is something parents will appreciate.

- **Do:** *Use social media correctly.* A challenge most practices have with social media is they choose a platform, usually Facebook, maybe Twitter, and that's all they use. Find out what your clients are using and go there. Are they on Instagram, Pinterest, Tumblr, LinkedIn? It would be wise to have a Social Media Chancellor or Buzz Ambassador for your company to help you keep up on where your clients are hanging out.

These are just a few principals to get a good referral program going in your practice. It would be a great idea to sit with your team and brainstorm more ideas that can work in your local area. The guidance of "Ask and you shall receive" is over 2,000 years old and it still rings true today. One thing I know for sure, every unasked-for referral is an automatic "no."

The Client is NOT Always Right

It's important to address something small business owners have a difficult time doing (mostly due to a scarcity mindset) but need to take more control over. Here it is: you get to choose your clients, which means you can also "un-choose" them.

A client routinely arrives at your office 30 minutes late for their scheduled appointments. When they arrive late, they still demand to be seen and receive service. This throws your whole day off, limits your flexibility, and forces you to be rushed, or even inconvenience other customers that were early or on time.

Old-school business practices, typically based upon fear of losing a customer, would tell you "the customer is always right". What do you think? Was that customer right?

You have to weigh a few things when dealing with this client.

> *What are the benefits of making this customer happy?*

> *What are the potential costs to your business and operations for trying to accommodate this client?*

Let's look at another situation.

You have a client that always demands a discount for your product or services. Every time they do business with you, they always haggle or pressure you for a concession. They pay late or don't pay at all until you write off or reduce the amount owed.

> *Is this customer right?*

> *Why would a business keep a customer like this?*

> *What would be the "right" thing to do?*

Customers are not always right.

As a company, you only have a limited amount of resources... hours, office space, equipment, money, etc. How much can you afford to spend in accommodating any one single client? It is true that it is different for every client and for every company, but no matter what, you can't stand by the mantra "the client is always right." There must be certain standards of conduct and client behavior that you require in order to do business. When customers routinely or grossly violate those standards, feel free to "fire" them as customers.

When or how you fire a client has to be considered on a case-by-case basis. To help out in that decision, here are three simple specifics that can lead to firing a customer.

1. When a client demands too much undue attention.

2. When a client becomes abusive or aggressive in communication towards you or your team members.

Money isn't everything. When a client won't work with you according to your expectations, don't do business with them.

I'm not suggesting that you stop trying to accommodate clients, but I encourage you to look at the big picture when dealing with customers that routinely eat up resources or that you simply can't accommodate.

Even the happiest place on earth, Disneyland, has a list of "un-invited" guests. If you become too disruptive or cause a problem, they will invite you to leave and not come back. Just ask Justin Bieber.

So what are you doing to create better relationships in your life? I'm going to assume that I've convinced you that relationship capital is the most important part of your business.

In a difficult situation, ask yourself — Do you want better relationships with yourself and your spouse, your team members and your clients?

Chapter Takeaway:

- People do business with people they know, like and trust.
- Sharing your story with your clients develops a stronger bond that naturally brings more clients toward your business.

"Gratitude for your employees is number one. Gratitude is the greatest magnet for other people. If you don't appreciate your employees, you are never going to develop leaders.

Number two is delegation. For me, delegation has given me the ability to grow as quickly as I have. I have to allow people to have successes and also have failures and to learn from them.

All of my leaders in all of my locations have made big screw ups. They've all had some big wins too, and so we all learn from them. But if you micromanage people and don't give them a chance to fail, they don't ever have a chance to learn.

If somebody is not willing to do business and treat people the way you would, then they are not right for your team. That was the hardest thing for me to learn. You have to be willing to terminate people who don't have your same values and don't represent your name or your mission statement well. It all has to be consistent across the board, especially if your name is on the building.

You put people in positions and put them under more pressure, they will either step up to the pressure or they will step out. Eventually, one of those two things will happen. If it doesn't happen fast enough, you have to let them go.

Team building is very important, gratitude for your team is of utmost importance, and then being able to let your team succeed and fail by delegating tasks to them and not micromanaging them.

Those are my three keys to success."

Dr. Jordan Cooper, DDS
Cooper Family Dentistry

PART FOUR

Excellence

EXCELLENCE

• •

"Excellence is not an act but a habit."

— Aristotle

The final section discussing the CORE will cover understanding how to strive for "Excellence" in your practice. Here we will break down three fundamentals necessary to achieve excellence. The only true way to achieve excellence in anything is to consistently keep growing.

Changing the culture you currently have into one of excellence is like dieting. Even though there are plenty of ways to lose the weight, nothing will work until you decide to make a commitment to change. Nothing short of your total commitment will do.

According to research by IBM, between 60 and 90 percent of organizational change initiatives fall flat. Just like going to the gym for a month will not result in lifetime fitness, making the changes that lead to excellence is a long process. It often means rewiring a company's fundamental DNA.

You now have a powerful outline that shows you that you can have the practice you want. When it comes to true change, however, none of it will matter if you don't follow the steps in this final section.

Although the roadmap to excellence varies, there seem to be three universal, fundamental strategies that all who have achieved success have included in their lives and business.

First is mentorship. From Tiger Woods to Warren Buffett, mentorship has been and always will be a foundation for achieving great things. We will break down the three stages of mentorship to use in your business so that you can achieve the excellence you seek.

Next is the power of continual learning. Those who have achieved excellence understand that if you are not growing, you are dying. They seek new information both in their field and elsewhere.

Last is the power of celebrating success. From simple fist pumps to lavish parties, anchoring into your psyche the positive emotion of having done a good job creates a desire to do it again. "Success begets success" as they say, and you will learn how to create a habit of it.

After learning the power of mentorship, continual learning, and finally, developing systems to celebrate your success, excellence will be a way of business, not just something you are seeking.

MENTORSHIP

● ●

"There is no lack of knowledge out there,
just a shortage of asking for help."

— *Unknown*

What do professional golfer Tiger Woods, Academy Award-winning actor Meryl Streep, Olympic snowboarder Sean White, billionaire fashion designer and Shark Tank 'shark' Damon John, Microsoft founder Bill Gates, President Barack Obama and just about every other celebrity, scholar, athlete and business mogul have in common when it comes to achieving excellence? Of course, the title of this chapter gives you the obvious answer. They all have coaches and mentors in their lives.

From some of the earliest thinkers and achievers like Socrates and Plato to modern business giants like Bill Gates and Oprah Winfrey, the importance of hiring a mentor is nothing new to those who want to achieve more in their lives or businesses. Most of you reading this have likely hired a mentor, coach or consultant for your business at some point. Some of you are perfectly happy with the mentors you have hired, while others of you may feel like you did not get what you hoped for.

No matter where you fall in the spectrum of satisfaction with your mentorship experience, this chapter is going to help clarify how to use mentorship in your business to achieve the best results.

From holding you accountable to being your biggest cheerleader, talking about the obvious benefits of hiring a mentor in your business would frankly be nothing new for a business book, and I don't think it would add any new value to your mindset. So, like most of the information in this book, I want to give you a different perspective in the power of mentoring in your business.

For starters, most people do not understand that if you really want to reach the next level of excellence in your business, simply hiring a mentor (no matter how good that mentor is) is not enough. Hiring a mentor is only the first phase of a great mentorship program. In order to take your practice to the next level, there are two more phases of mentorship you will want to adopt.

In this chapter we will discuss the importance of (and what to look for in) a great mentor for your practice. Then, we will discover the power of becoming a mentor yourself, until finally discussing an area which most small practices don't do enough of – the power of creating a mentorship program within your practice.

Let's start with the mentors you hire and dissect the attributes you need to personally have in order to create the results you want and the attributes you need to look for in a mentor so that you don't waste your time with the wrong ones.

Mentors You Hire

Henry Ford had a problem that his electrical engineers couldn't solve. A gigantic generator stopped working correctly, costing his automobile company thousands of dollars every day. So he called mathematical genius Charles Steinmetz at the Edison Company for some assistance. In the 1920s Mr. Steinmetz's discoveries changed the way engineers thought about circuits and machines and made him the most recognized name in electricity for decades.

Agreeing to help, Steinmetz arrived at the plant a few days later and quickly rejected any assistance offered by those who had been working on the problem previously. His only request was a notebook, pencil and a cot to sleep on. Over the next two days and nights Steinmetz listened intently to the generator while scribbling various calculations on the notepad.

On the second night, he stopped writing, asked for a ladder, positioned himself under the generator, climbed up the side of the generator and paused. Then, he made a simple chalk mark on the side of the generator wall where he was perched.

When he climbed down, he told Ford's engineers to remove the plate at the point where he had made the mark and replace sixteen windings from the field coil. Although skeptical, they did as requested, replaced the windings, and then powered up the generator. It performed to perfection.

The generator was up and running again and the company was quickly back to its normal production schedule. A grateful Mr. Ford was thrilled... that is, until a week later when he received the invoice from Mr. Steinmetz in the amount of $10,000. Although Ford acknowledged Steinmetz's success and was grateful to have his company up and running again, he balked at the figure he saw in front of him. Frustrated, he demanded an itemized bill.

Steinmetz's response? The next day Mr. Ford received an itemized invoice for his services that read:

Making chalk mark on generator: $1

Knowing where to make mark: $9,999

Ford paid the bill.

At first glance, it might be difficult to see why I chose this story as a mentorship example. I agree that the final lesson is a powerful one, but I chose this story as both an argument on the importance of hiring a mentor as well as an illustration to the necessary qualities you want in one.

Let's use this story to examine the various mentor qualities you will want to seek in a mentor as well as the mentee qualities you will want to develop in order to produce the best mentor experience possible.

The first takeaway from the story is a lesson Mr. Ford teaches about the need to be teachable. We all need to realize how important it is to ask for help if we want a different result than we currently have.

The truth is, you could hire the best mentor in the world and they could have all the qualities we are about to discover. If you are not honestly willing to be taught, though, you're wasting your time.

There is no arguing that Henry Ford was a smart man, even a genius. I believe no one would question that his engineers were also very smart and capable men. Likewise, you are obviously an intelligent and capable professional. However, just like the malfunctioning generator was slowing down Mr. Ford and his company, all of us have areas in our lives that are slowing us down or not performing well.

Malfunctioning areas are costing you in a variety of ways, from money and peace of mind to your relationships or your health.

In Ford's case it was money — a lot of it. Although it does not say so in the story, I am sure Mr. Ford and his engineers spent a considerable amount of time trying to fix the problem on their own. They might have even been a bit prideful about admitting they were at a loss as to how to fix it. But just like the doctor who has tried and tried to implement a specific strategy or suggest a different way to perform a procedure in his practice, only to have his team still not be able to get it right, Ford and his team had to humble themselves for the good of the company and admit what they didn't know. That brings us to our next quality...

MENTEE QUALITY #1: *Admit What You Don't Know*

Mr. Ford found someone who was not attached to the challenge, but was capable of finding a solution to help.

Having someone from outside your business or even your industry, someone who is not directly related to the problem, whose only focus is to look at the challenge from a different point of view, can help pinpoint areas you might not have thought about or seen before.

Mr. Ford did not ask for just anyone's help. He called in the best person he could find. Steinmetz was not just another engineer. He was not even in the automobile industry. He was **The Man** when it came to electrical engineering.

Are you following Mr. Ford's example? Are you seeking out the best mentor you can find with the ability and track record to give you the results you need?

MENTEE QUALITY #2: *Seek the Best Help, No Matter Where it Might Come From*

The qualities you want to seek out in a mentor are revealed in Mr. Steinmetz's actions. He bypassed listening to what the Ford engineers thought the problem was and went right to work listening to the generator in order to find the problem. Rather than spending his time with the people who might cloud his mind with all the things they'd already tried and failed at, thus skewing his perception, he only wanted to observe the subject, listen to what it was "saying" and ask questions through his own computations.

This might sound strange at first, but in my experience, great mentors are not interested in listening to all the various reasons why things aren't working, especially from those who have already tried to help. Do they want to know what you think the problem is? Of course they do. They probably even want to know what you have tried in the past. However, great mentors know, in most cases, that what you say is the problem is not really the problem. When asked what the problem is, most people like to point out the failed result and not the actual problem.

When I visit an office and ask a team member, office managers and doctor about the biggest problems they face in the business, they rarely tell me the actual problem; they tell me the result.

> *"I feel like I am continually having to retrain my team on the same thing I taught them just 6 months ago."*

> *"I paid good money to have a consultant come in to help us with the billing, but it was too difficult to change what our clients were comfortable, with so we went back to the old ways."*

> *"Our clients just don't do what we ask."*

> *"The doctor has not given bonuses in months."*

> *"Our staff doesn't get along."*

By now, with all you have learned about culture and leadership in this book, you can see that these are just complaints about the result, not the problem.

Honestly, I don't expect them to know what the actual problem is. If they really knew it, they wouldn't need me. I am just gathering information so that I can uncover the real problem and give them a specific solution.

I imagine the engineers would have taken up precious time by telling Steinmetz all the reasons they thought the generator was not working. Worse, if Steinmetz had accepted their help in the process, they would have most likely tainted his focus by questioning his method that they did not understand, arguing that his idea was not the way it had been done before or waste his time with all the reasons why his methods wouldn't work.

We are all reason-making machines. It's easier to come up with a reason why something is the way it is or why it won't work than it is to admit we were wrong or ignorant of another option. Especially when someone we really don't know is trying to tell us how to improve our business or ourselves. Typically our first reaction to anyone pointing out what we are doing wrong or could be doing better is to go into defense mode. Even if we logically understand that the person is there to help us. Even if we were the ones to hire that person to help, we can take their direction as a personal attack. Especially if we have a long-established habit of doing things a certain way.

Steinmetz knew he would be able to better serve his client if he went in with no preconceived notions, and only the basic information about the company's problem. This allowed him to investigate the problem on his own and create new possible solutions.

MENTOR TRAIT TO SEEK #1: *Look for the problem, don't listen to reasons. Ask questions and, most of all, listen.*

Mr. Steinmetz took his time. He kept focus. He didn't just sacrifice his time; he sacrificed his comfort in order to find the problem he was seeking. He quite literally slept next to the problem. He took his time and after two full days of listening to the problem, the esteemed mentor climbed the ladder and made his mark. Then, with confidence, he told Mr. Ford exactly what to do to fix his problem generator.

We know of his confidence because he didn't just suggest that the engineers look in a general area and start replacing windings until they found the right amount. He did not give them a roundabout number of windings to replace; he said they needed to replace sixteen, at an exact point. His patience and labored effort in listening allowed him to pinpoint the exact area and the exact systems that were not working correctly.

Many of us seek the quick fix to getting what we say we want in life. How can I lose weight quickly? What is the shortcut to finding wealth? We are programmed to want the fastest result in the shortest amount of time. Some mentors will even be willing to tell you they can fix your problems in no time at all, with zero effort on your part. While some positive changes are found by going "cold turkey", the fact is real change takes time. You cannot have the beach body you want in just 30 days, especially if you've spent the last 40 treating it like a garbage can.

Likewise, the problems most people are experiencing in life and in business have been developed over a long period of time, so be willing to be patient and honor the journey it will take to gain new and better results.

MENTOR TRAIT TO SEEK #2: Real, lasting solutions do not come in quick fix packages.

A skeptical group of engineers did exactly what the mathematician said. This is a critical point when working with your mentor. You have to be willing to do what the mentor asks and trust he or she can see something you can't. It's not easy for most people. When someone tells us what to do, we tend to be skeptical, especially if it's like the windings hidden behind a wall, something we can't physically see in front of us. And because you can't see it, you doubt it.

Of all the places where I have seen companies, marriages and people sabotage their success, this step is the most common. I give my client the solution to their problem. The problem they said they were desperate to solve and, at the time, were willing to do anything it took to fix it. I tell them exactly what to do and even explain the likelihood of the desired outcome if it's done. Then when it comes to actually implementing the solution, they have "a better idea." I am not talking about how they can improve upon the suggestion. I'm talking about a complete morphing of what I know will help. Because of this "better idea," a majority of the time, the end result is frustration and disappointment. The problem is still there and worse, they now have evidence as to why the suggestion they never actually fully embraced won't work for them. Negating the fact that it was the final fatal flaw of their "better idea," which created the unsuccessful result.

For a variety of reasons, we all sabotage our success in some degree or another. Often, that sabotage is because of the level of difficulty it will take to implement the suggestion. Sometimes it's due to the amount of time and effort it will take. For others it's the fact that although they say they want change, they are actually really comfortable in the pain they know and are used to. They would rather avoid going through the pain they don't know and experiencing the uncomfortable process of actually changing.

Why is that? If we say we want something and even hire someone to show us the way, why would we then consciously stop ourselves from achieving it?

Putting faith in someone else's suggestion is hard for many of us. Especially if it involves something or someone we care about. It's your business, your marriage, your friendship, your health, and having to take a chance and change what you are comfortable doing based upon the suggestion of someone who is not and cannot be as attached to the outcome as you are is difficult.

We stress over thoughts like, "What if my mentor is wrong? What will my employees, colleague and family think of me?" These are normal concerns.

However, in order to get a different result, you have to do something different. You have to be willing to do hard things and get out of your comfort zone. There are no shortcuts. It is the only way you will actually make the changes you want to make in your business and life.

MENTEE QUALITY #3: *Don't sabotage your success with your "better idea." Get uncomfortable and be willing to take a leap of faith.*

The good news is that when you believe you've hired the right person to guide you, someone who is in alignment with your core values, who would never suggest you do anything immoral or illegal, you owe it to yourself to be like the skeptical engineers — be uncomfortable and do what the mentor tells you to do.

The result, honestly, is unknown. However, the chances of experiencing what Mr. Ford and his engineers did, getting the generator running better than before are much higher when you bring the right mentors into your life.

Now that you are armed with the qualities you need to get the most out of your mentoring experience, it's time to learn how to solidify the lessons you will learn and create a true needle-mover in your life.

The Principle that Changes the Game

There is one more lesson to learn from the Ford generator story. It's in the value you put on your services and the services of others. Access this special training, plus other bonus content in *The Path to the Propreneur*. Get it today at thepracticecure.com.

Becoming the Mentor

Have you noticed that there has been an upsurge over the last 10 to 20 years in professional mentors? Whatever they call themselves (life coaches, life designers, business consultants, the list goes on), there are many names for this seemingly new profession. There are literally mentors and coaches for everything from what to eat to how to work out, to dating and how to organize your closet. The mentoring profession has invaded our society like never before over the last decade or so. Why is that? More importantly, why is it necessary and what does it have to do with your business? Shannon and I were discussing this one day a few years ago and she had an interesting philosophy that I think answers these questions.

If you go back a few generations and look at the life-learning methods of most people in our society, the lessons that were taught were typically passed down from one generation to the next. What your great-great grandfather learned about life, business, and being a father or husband was passed down to your great grandfather, then he passed it on to your grandfather, and so forth. The same cycle happened with the female side of the family. Why is that? Families were not as transient as we are today. In most cases back then, entire generations of relatives lived in the same town or area of the country. This would create a natural cycle of passing on life lessons, wisdom and know-how, providing a support system for just about any challenge or need.

Mom, grandma or even aunt was the life coach for new moms who needed to learn how to balance the needs of a home. Grandpa and dad were the business coach that would train you on how to be a better leader, business owner and member of the community.

However, over the last few decades we have become a much more transient people. Moving away from your hometown to attend college or accept a job opportunity in another state is almost a right of passage. With the ease and relatively inexpensive cost of being able to hop on a plane and fly across the country in a matter of hours, we justify the fact that we can live our life away from home, but still be connected to it when necessary, but at what cost?

Even though we have the Internet and cell phones that actually give us immediate access, the adage "out of sight, out of mind" is a reality when it comes to whom you now look to for advice. So we seek out grandpa and grandma-like wisdom elsewhere.

Of course, there are other variables to this surge in mentorship. The way we do most things, from business to parenting, have definitely changed in our world. It's true that most grandparents and even parents today probably wouldn't be the best resource for how to effectively run an online marketing company or structure a business where your employees are based in another country.

This has resulted in our giving up that wisdom of past generations we used to have easy and immediate access to. No longer do we have the kitchen sit-downs with grandpa about how to better get along with our wife, how to deal with difficult employees and the meaning of life. We still need and seek that wisdom. We now just seek it from a larger pool of available resources.

This is not a criticism of the mentoring upsurge. Obviously, I make my living as one of those advice-givers. It's just an observation and possible explanation as to why. It's also an opportunity for your business.

Interestingly, in the private practice field the idea of mentorship is not anything new. I have interviewed multiple professionals who said they entered into their field because their father or grandfather was in the same profession. One client of mine is a fourth generation chiropractor. However, that generational passing of the professional torch, if you will, is also becoming increasingly rare.

That is where your opportunity lies.

One of the secrets of great leadership is the desire to become a great mentor. There are three main reasons that taking the responsibility of mentorship upon you is good for your business.

1. You have an opportunity to shape the next generation and keep the integrity of your profession intact by passing on your own hard-earned wisdom.
2. You gain the insight of someone with fresh eyes, as covered in the previous chapter.
3. By teaching your skill, it forces you to continually sharpen your own axe.

It is the wise graduate who seeks out a practice where he or she can become an associate not just to get real-world experience in the field (or even to buy out the owner as soon as possible), but more importantly so that he can learn from a great and experienced mentor. It's also the wise practice owner who doesn't just look for a good worker bee to lift part of the patient load from him, he will have a desire to become a mentor and coach to the associate, so that he can solidify all the years of experience and pass on the years of wisdom gained.

Mentoring younger professionals is just one way you can keep your axe sharpened. With the information you have learned in this book alone, you can reach out and help a fellow colleague. Add that to all of your years of practical learning, both the successes and the missteps, and you can offer to teach CE classes, speak at local associations, study groups and conventions.

You are a fountain of knowledge and wisdom, and I believe you owe it to yourself and to your profession to seek out mentorship opportunities. I can promise you that the more you do, the more you will grow. Buddha said it better than I can when he said, "If you light a lantern for another it will also brighten your own way."

Exercise: *Qualities of a Mentor*

Take a few moments and write down all of your great qualities that you feel could help someone else out in life. Throw modesty and feelings of not wanting to brag out the window for just a moment and go for it. (It's okay. No one is looking.) I want you to see that you have a lot to offer others if you really think about it.

_____

_____

_____

_____

_____

_____

_____

That wasn't so bad, was it? You might have even enjoyed it just a little bit.

How many qualities you listed are reflective of the qualities mentioned in the previous chapter?

Now see how many of your qualities match up with the following list of attributes of great mentors:

- A desire to share your knowledge or expertise.
- Positive attitude even when facing challenges.
- A spirit of curiosity.
- Personally interested in others.
- Enthusiastic.
- The heart of a teacher and the mind of a student.
- Gives honest guidance and constructive feedback.
- Respected by others and shows respect.
- A goal-setter.
- Learns from mistakes.
- Values others' opinions.
- Motivates others.
- Strives to set a good example.

Although there are more that can and should be mentioned, these and the ones you wrote down are a good place to start on your mentoring journey.

Mentoring You Create

"Tell me and I forget, teach me and I may remember,
involve me and I learn."

— *Benjamin Franklin*

If you are like many professionals I talk to, you often feel overwhelmed, stressed and inundated by all the moving parts that go into running a business. Your brain never seems to shut off with the constant reminder that the business will rise or fall upon your efforts alone. Although understandable, due to the fact that your name is above the door, the weight of that pressure can actually become lighter if you embrace the idea of creating a mentorship culture within your practice.

The reason you are feeling those emotions is due to the fact that you think you're alone. Until you learn to create a mentoring culture in your practice, you will always be managing your business instead of leading it. It brings us back to the principle of working *in* your business instead of working *on* your business.

In the final phase of mentoring to excellence, you will learn the principals of creating an effective mentorship program that will help you do just that. When you divide up the tasks and create systems for each area of your business with a specific method of communication, accountability, and personal ownership, not only does your feeling of burden become lighter, your business will run more efficiently and better than you can currently imagine.

Building a mentorship program within a company is nothing new. As a matter of fact, in the competitive business environment they are becoming quite prevalent. Fortune 500 companies like IBM, AT&T, Hewlett-Packard and Costco all have integrated mentorship programs.

A true mentorship program goes beyond the simple cross-training efforts some private practice owners try to implement, usually with minimal results. It involves a specific program that is first designed to meet the needs of every department within your practice, and then, the needs of the practice as a whole.

Creating a mentoring culture within in your practice is a process that requires focus, discipline, and patience. Due to the very nature of the program, it will never be finished. It is a continual work in progress. The process of creating, improving, shifting and then re-creating is ongoing. When done correctly it will last beyond the tenure of everyone in the practice... even you. It demands ongoing learning and feedback to achieve desired results. When mentoring is embedded in an organizational culture that values continuous learning, which we will talk about in the next chapter, it increases the chances of long-term sustainability. To be ultimately successful, mentoring programs must include flexibility, clarity, and feedback.

So what is the formula to a successful internal practice-mentoring program?

First, find the "rock stars" in your company. If you have what I call a core team, typically an office manager, treatment coordinator, marketing director or the like, that is the first place to start. I would hope that any individuals in those positions are the leaders in the practice. However, the sad reality I know is that is not always the case. So who are the members, that are constantly engaged, excited to be there and striving for excellence. These might be team members who have been around for a while but that also is not always the case. Do not get caught in the trap of choosing the veteran employee over the talent just because the veteran has been there longer and you don't want to hurt feelings.

If you don't feel you have any true rock stars, it's time to announce that you are looking for them so that they have the chance to step up and show you what they have to offer.

Dr. A was sure his dental assistant Karen was not going to last much longer in his practice. He had just recently become the sole owner of a practice after five years of buying out his predecessor. Karen had been in a member of the team for all of those five years and to be honest, he was never really impressed with her work ethic. She did her job well enough, but that was it. When it came to going the extra mile and looking for ways to be productive between patients, she definitely did not put in the effort. Until the buyout was complete, he did not have control of the hiring process. So when we first met, Karen was someone who Dr. A had in his sights as a possible team member he was going to "love into another company".

If you would have asked Dr. A who the "rock-stars" were on his team when we first started the program, Karen's name would most definitely not have been on the list.

However, just as in this book, part of my program he underwent was to create a specific set of core values for the company, and then, once solidified, ask every member of the team if they would commit to all of the values, everyday. He did, and something interesting happened. Karen started to step up and act differently. She was more engaged, involved and she found ways to be productive. She became the rock star the doctor was looking for.

If you don't feel you have any real rock stars, set up the expectation and tell them what you are looking for. You might be surprised who steps up their game.

Once you have found your leaders, work with them to create the mentoring program for each department.

A successful program will include:

- **A specific desired outcome or goal.** It's not a goal unless it is written down.

- **Time frames or benchmarks to track progress.** If we don't know what the finish line looks like, how will we know if we have arrived?

- **Ongoing feedback and evaluation.** The more frequent the conversation about the journey, the easier it is to keep everyone on track and recover from missteps.

- **Welcome failure.** Just as in leadership qualities, you want your team to know it is better to have gone for it and failed than it is to never have tried at all.

- **Extra education and training.** This might include workshops, conventions, and outside resources like consultants and coaches.

- **Reporting both in the department and to the practice as a whole.** This allows for everyone to get involved and support the process.

- **Rewards or bonuses.** As you know by now, this is not always financially based; use your team members Support Styles to create incentives for a job well done.

It *must* be duplicable. You are not looking for unique systems that can only be performed by a select group of people. You want a program that can be easily taught to anyone who joins your team.

I am sure you can see by now the power of creating a strong mentoring program in your practice. It will help you take the burden off your back, give you peace of mind and further create that strong feeling of team.

In closing, remember that successful mentoring programs also are tied to something larger than just a program. When mentoring is included as a part of the culture you are creating, it is not perceived as an add-on to what is already in place; rather, it is part of the practice's DNA. A powerful and successful mentoring program will create a shared understanding and vocabulary within your team that fits naturally with the organization's values, mission, and goals.

Exercise: *Mentoring Brainstorm*

What mentoring programs would you like to start in your practice?

_____

_____

_____

_____

_____

_____

_____

_____

_____

Who are the leaders or "rock stars" you think can help you?

_____

_____

_____

_____

_____

_____

_____

_____

When are you going to start your first mentoring program?

_____

_____

_____

_____

_____

_____

_____

Chapter Takeaway:

- It's important to ask for help if you want a different result. Be willing to seek help for anything you don't have an answer for.

- Recognize that there are no quick fixes if you desire lasting results. Lasting success takes hard work and determination.

- You are a fountain of knowledge and wisdom. You owe it to yourself and to your profession to seek out mentorship opportunities. By mentoring others, you'll grow as well. *"If you light a lantern for another, it will also brighten your own way."*

ENCOURAGE LEARNING

● ●

"Those people who develop the ability to continuously acquire new and better forms of knowledge that they can apply to their work and to their lives will be the movers and shakers in our society for the indefinite future."

— *Brian Tracy*

The quote above just about sums up this entire chapter.

Creating a culture of continuous learning with you as a leader, and with the members of your team, is essential to the success of your business. Encouraging the learning of new concepts, new ideas, and new procedures not only have the benefit of keeping your company on an upward trend; it also combats the natural occurrence of entropy in your practice.

In a nutshell, the Principal of Entropy states that no matter the company, product or program, systems will naturally break down over time. It's inevitable. The only alternative is to continually improve, refine, revise, and enhance your systems; thus the reason I've focused so much on mentorship within your practice.

The same goes for people.

You and every employee you have will improve in specifically the skills you use every day. They will develop competencies and efficiencies around the systems and procedures that they perform daily as part of their positions. What they won't do is naturally develop the skills they don't use every day, but that could benefit their performance in their job.

Think about what you've been doing through this entire book. You've learned various skill sets, including sales and customer service. You've learned about leadership, delegation, decision-making, and relationship skills, all of which don't necessarily improve your ability to perform a medical procedure, but they do enhance your experience, the interactions you have with others, your customers' satisfaction, and your overall profitability. Gaining skills and knowledge is key to the growth and continued enhancement of your office.

A 2010 article by the American Society of Clinical Oncology stated that *"[As a leader]... you have an important role in staff development: establishing its priority, encouraging it by example, and supporting it in your attitude and budget. The truth is that if staff education and development are not a priority for the physicians who own the practice, they will not be a priority for anyone under them."*

This quote is primarily talking about continual in-house education, which is definitely needed, but what about the benefits of encouraging your team members to get education and training on a subject that is not directly related to their jobs? What would be the benefit of that for you? Turns out, there are quite a few.

Most, if not all, of the companies I have mentioned in this book so far have some sort of a continual education program as part of their company culture. From in-house libraries of business and motivational books that can be checked out anytime to after-hours study groups, having these programs in place communicates two powerful messages to employees. First, on a small scale, is says that the company actually cares about the employees' growth, and second, it makes a more extreme statement that they are okay with employees actually outgrowing current positions, even if that means the employees might leave them someday.

The media and publishing company Mindvalley actually has a specific program that encourages its employees to learn a new skill. It's called the 45/5 rule.

Out of the typical 45 hours an employee works every week at Mindvalley, they are not just encouraged to spend five hours a week studying a new skill that is unrelated to their job position, they are required and paid to do so. Employees are provided a massive library of coaching and training materials to help the employees learn through special seminars where they pay to have educators brought in to train the employees on various topics.

On top of that, every employee has an unlimited budget on Amazon so that they can buy any books they want. They encourage entrepreneurship through training and mentoring programs. This unique program has actually helped Mindvalley team members grow immensely in their careers and lives. Close to 25% of everyone Mindvalley has hired has become an entrepreneur within two years. Twelve percent actually end up becoming financially backed by Mindvalley.

Maybe you're thinking, "Dino, It's hard enough to find great employees. Why would I encourage or pay for the possibility of them to leave me?"

What if you looked at it another way? Aside from the obvious bonuses of employee loyalty and retention because they know you care about their growth, or the innate improvement of team morale, the increase in efficiency and job competency, it will also reflect on one of the best marketing tools you could ask for... patient satisfaction.

When your employees feel you care enough about them, they tend to have a more positive attitude, be more focused on taking care of your business, more willing to go the extra mile, and treat your patients better all-around. This means your patients will be happier with your service, think more highly of you and be more apt to tell their friends about how awesome your service is. In the end it is a huge marketing tool to bring more clients into your business. It also brings the added bonus of attracting more talented team members who want to work with you.

When you show your team members that you care about their continual education, you show them an even deeper level of commitment to strengthening your relationships with them.

As a side effect of adding educational opportunities, one practice has also seen an attraction of new and talented people who literally show up at his office resume in hand, asking how they can work for him. People show up and say, "I've seen what you're doing here and I want to be a part of it."

There are three primary reasons why implementing a continual education program with your team will help you and your practice grow:

1. Learning takes you from competent to good to great.
2. Learning supports performance.
3. Learning leads to success.

From Competent, to Good, to Great

A little boy once wanted to learn to swim. His parents took him to the local swimming pool and enrolled him with an instructor. After a few weeks, he had learned the basics of swimming and could perform a few strokes, travelling a few feet before stopping. His parents cheered and clapped, but the boy thought that he could still do better.

He kept going to swimming classes and after a few more weeks, he was able to swim across the little pool that he was learning in. His parents cheered and clapped, but the boy thought that he could still do better.

After a while he was eventually able to turn and swim back the other way. After a few more months, he was able to complete a few laps of the pool in one effort. His parents cheered and clapped, but the boy thought that he could still do better.

He started to enter swimming competitions and eventually won his first race. His parents cheered and clapped, but the boy thought that he could still do better.

One day, he decided the pool's distance was not enough, so he went to the ocean and swam from the beach to a pier a few hundred meters away. His parents cheered and clapped, but the boy thought that he could still do better.

He entered an ocean race that was a couple of kilometers in length and won with his first attempt. His parents cheered and clapped, but the boy thought that he could still do better.

So he stood on the beach and looked out over the ocean, out to the horizon beyond. He wondered what the limits were on what he could achieve and whether he had reached them yet. He aspired to something greater and set about planning how to achieve it.

Learning is the fuel in the engine of our development. We may already have skills that learning will enhance. We may completely lack skills and learning will introduce things to us. In other ways, we may be great at something, and a little more knowledge can take us to world-class levels.

It doesn't matter where you start, just that you are improving.

The story above, although fairly straightforward, illustrates how a desire to improve, grow, and develop over time can take us from the most basic of skills to mastery. You undoubtedly have experienced that in your own journey. The path from a confused freshman in college to the late night study groups in your professional training to where you are now has only happened because you, like that little boy, had a desire for mastery.

Creating the environment for continual education within your team will invite them to seek that mastery as well. After all, don't you want an entire team who is focused on being great – not just good – at what they do?

If you have not done so already, it's important to ask yourself this question: "Do I really want a team full of 'competent' or even 'good' people? Or do I want a team full of **great** people who are striving for mastery?"

If you picked up this book to learn how to unload some of your stress and frustration, then I hope it is clear by now that one of the easiest ways to do that (as well as create more happiness, mental clarity and profit) is to hire people who are always looking for the "horizon" like the little boy, not people who are content staying in the pool.

Hiring competent people and expecting good results will never produce the vision for your company that you say you want. If you feel you have hired good talent, the easiest way to help them become great is by first offering them the opportunity to become great.

In his book *Good to Great: Why Some Companies Make the Leap... and Others Don't*, author James C. Collins explains why good is not good enough: "Good is the enemy of great. And that is one of the key reasons why we have so little that becomes great. We don't have great schools, principally because we have good schools. We don't have great government, principally because we have good government. Few people attain great lives, in large part because it is just so easy to settle for a good life."

And you might not have a great practice because you have a good one.

It's my belief that you are actually doing a disservice to yourself, your team members, your community and your profession when you allow for anything but greatness in your practice. Once again, Mr. Collins states it better than I could:

> *"Letting the wrong people hang around is unfair to all the right people, as they inevitably find themselves compensating for the inadequacies of the wrong people. Worse, it can drive away the best people. Strong performers are intrinsically motivated by performance, and when they see their efforts impeded by carrying extra weight, they eventually become frustrated."*

What great talent are you missing out on in your practice because you are willing to settle for good talent?

Learning Supports Performance

Once upon a time, a very strong woodcutter asked for a job from a timber merchant, and he got it. The pay was great and so were the work conditions. For that reason, the eager woodcutter was determined to do his best.

His boss gave him an axe and showed him the area where he was supposed to work.

The first day, the woodcutter brought 18 trees down. "Congratulations," the boss said. "Keep it up!"

Very motivated by the boss's words, the woodcutter tried harder the next day, but he could only bring down 15 trees. The third day he tried even harder, but he could only bring down 10 trees. Day after day he was bringing down less and less trees.

"I must be losing my strength," the woodcutter thought. He went to the boss and apologized, saying that he could not understand what was going on.

"When was the last time you sharpened your axe?" the boss asked.

"Sharpen? I had no time to sharpen my axe. I have been very busy trying to cut trees..."

The story of sharpening the axe is not a new one, and I am sure you have heard one version or another of the parable. However, instead of seeing yourself as the woodcutter, what if you saw yourself as the boss of the woodcutter?

What if the boss would have taught the woodcutter about the importance of sharpening the axe earlier? What if he had taught him from the very beginning? The woodcutter wouldn't have become frustrated; instead, he would have continued to feel productive and excited about his accomplishments, and he would have kept producing a high amount of cut trees with no lag in the quality of work.

When you help your team members sharpen their axes, you, like the boss of the woodcutter, will get more out of them and it will ultimately benefit your bottom line.

As an exercise, think of all the ways you can support your team in furthering their education and how that might benefit you. Brainstorm for just a moment how you can help them sharpen their axes.

_____

_____

_____

_____

_____

_____

_____

Learning Leads to Success

"Good judgment comes from experience. Experience usually comes from bad decisions."
-Anonymous

Earlier in the book, I talked about the importance of being willing to "focus on failure". When it comes to creating true success in your practice, you have to be willing to create an environment where failing with the focus of learning is encouraged. The benefits to your staff, their attitudes, and confidence are substantially improved by adopting that as part of your culture. Learning from mistakes improves performance in unexpected ways.

There once was a potter who was teaching pottery making to a class of 20 students. As an experiment, the potter split the class into two groups, giving each group a simple, yet different objective.

His hope was to teach his class something about learning and its relationship to creativity and failure.

For group 1, the objective he gave was for each student to make one perfect pot.

For group 2, his objective was for each student to use up 100 pounds of clay.

The first group struggled, working on the one pot days on end. Most failed to get it right.

The second group went through a lot of clay and failed often. But through failure they learned, iterated and perfected their technique. By the end most had several perfect pots.

Though the group focused on perfection took longer, they never achieved it because they did not make room for growth through error. Of course, the second group had more freedom and therefore were able to learn from their mistakes until they could produce the desired results.

Mastery, enhanced performance and the likelihood of success all seem like powerful reasons to implement a culture of continual learning that will directly benefit your company, do they not?

There is one more reason I hope you take this idea to heart for yourself, personally.

As a leader, mentor and example to your team, I believe when you have the spirit of continual learning in your own life and you learn new skills in addition to the ones connected to your everyday profession, it will make you a better practitioner. I challenge you to find a subject or skill to learn that has no direct effect on your business and see how it makes you better.

I have personally taken this section to heart in my own life.

As a boy, my mom signed me up for piano lessons. I hated it. I still remember cursing the fact that I had to ride my bike a mile down the road to the teacher's house. I was not upset in the slightest when my mom could not afford the lessons anymore and I had to quit.

But not knowing how to play the piano became a huge regret in my life. For years, I dreamt about being able to sit down at a piano and play a song. When I got married, my wife inherited a piano and for years I would look at it wishing I knew how to play. Every year I would think, *someday I'll learn*. And things always ended up getting in the way... until last year.

I was teaching this concept to a client when they called me on it. They asked me what I had been learning that had nothing to do with my profession. I was stuck. I was called out and had no response. Right then and there, I made a commitment to both the client and myself that I was going to live what I was preaching.

Ever since then, every Tuesday morning I have a standing appointment with Art, my piano teacher. I love the challenge. I love driving my family crazy with my plunking away the same simple tunes (It's interesting how Pop Goes The Weasel can unnerve teenagers). Most of all I can honestly say that activating the parts of my brain that require me to connect my hand-eye coordination has also helped me in areas of my business, from more easily dissecting and connecting concepts that can help my clients to just being more creative in my use of time throughout my day.

I have enjoyed it so much that I have recently added another creative outlet to my learning behavior. (Zumba, anyone?)

Chapter Takeaway:

- Hiring competent people and expecting great results will never produce the vision for your company that you say you want. If you feel you have hired good talent, the easiest way to help them become great is by first offering them the opportunity to become great.

- Learning takes you from competent to good to great.

- Learning supports performance. You must sharpen your axe in order to remain effective at your job.

- Learning leads to success. By expanding your horizons, you are able to tap into more creativity.

CELEBRATE SUCCESS

*"The more you praise and celebrate your life,
the more there is in life to celebrate."*

— *Oprah Winfrey*

Have you ever known anyone who seems to find success in every situation? Ever admired sports stars, celebrities and great business leaders, wondering how they come by so much success, with what looks like very little effort? Logically you know they have had to work for it to some capacity, but you still are amazed at the level and frequency of success they achieve. I'm not talking about the ones who've literally had their success handed to them on a platter aka inheritance. They have very little to teach you. I'm talking about the ones who just exude success... the ones who seem to achieve success on autopilot.

What's their secret? They have created the habit of success. They have trained their brains to be attracted to success. Success to them is not a secret or an accident; it's a system. One very important yet simple process of that system that you can start to adopt is to start celebrating success.

Our final lesson in this book is probably the most overlooked by most people. In truth this lesson is a reflection of one of the first lesson taught — mindset. The act of celebrating success can have an incredibly powerful effect on your business, your team and yourself and the more you create a mindset of success the more you will undoubtedly find it.

When we get into the habit of celebrating success, even the small things, we train our brains, like those automatically successful people, to seek out success in our daily life.

We've all heard the old adage "success breeds success", but is this really true? As it turns out, it is, and has been scientifically proven!

A group of researchers from the State University of New York, the Institute for Advanced Computational Science, and University College of London (meaning some REALLY smart guys) wanted to put this adage to the test. The process involved rewarding 200-500 random people in various ways. They either contributed funding for a proposed product on Kickstarter, provided an endorsement for a person's professional work, gave an award for dedication to a community group, or provided signatures for a social or political campaign.

What they found was that the people given support were up to 31% more likely to receive support from others. "Success promoted success regardless of merit, talent, aptitude, or social networks."

There were other findings from the study, but the main finding was that "a single initial success may be sufficient to trigger a self-propelling cascade of success!!"

How then do we go about training our brains to seek after the success we want to replicate? We have to create the habit of celebrating every success. From the big public accomplishments to the small private ones, the more we celebrate them, the more our brains will form the habit of seeking them.

We will discuss more effective ways of anchoring the habit in a moment. For now know that it doesn't have to be a huge thing, just something that anchors the good feeling in your mind. A simple fist bump with a friend or a fist pump by yourself consistently performed when you do something good is enough to create the habit. For some it's even just a process of simple self-talk that creates the habit.

Nine months before the 1984 Olympics, Gymnast Bart Connor tore his bicep muscle and most experts believed that he would never make it back in time to compete at the Olympics. Not only did he make it back, he won TWO gold medals.

When he was being interviewed after his achievements, he was asked how he did it. Bart thanked his parents. He explained, "Every night before bed my parents would ask me what my success was. So I went to bed a success every night of my life. I woke up every morning a success. When I was injured before the Olympics, I knew I was going to make it back because I was a success every day of my life."

Bart's parents planted a very important seed in his head at a young age. They didn't ask him if he had any success he would like to report, they asked him what his success were that day. The difference being, that for most of us, when we are asked if we have had any successes, we tend to discount them or think of them as no big deal, thus missing the opportunity to recognize them. When Mr. and Mrs. Connor asked him to tell them what his success was for that day, it made Bart seek and recognize his success. I am sure there were days where his success was something seemingly simple or even expected as an athlete in training, like making it through a routine or not giving up on a new move. Yet, having to search for the success everyday created a mindset and created habits that encouraged success throughout the day. In the end, succeeding was just a part of Bart's DNA.

In my live marriage training course, I will ask couples to spend time writing down their successes in life. I give them examples to write that range from the simple "We bought our first house" and "We made it through the teenage years" to the more extreme, such as "I beat cancer" or "We survived the death of a child." They spend about ten minutes working on the project, writing down all the success they can think of.

Then I invite a volunteer up to the front of the room. I tell the audience that in a moment they are going to have the chance to share their successes with the rest of the group. Before they do that, I demonstrate how that is going to look.

I ask the volunteers to announce one of the successes they have on their list. They proceed to humbly and meekly follow my instructions and report the one they are most proud of. I listen intently to their success and when they finish speaking I quickly rush up to them and yell at the top of my voice, "OH MY GOODNESS! THAT IS THE MOST AMAZING THING I HAVE EVER HEARD! OF COURSE YOU DID THAT BECAUSE YOU ARE AN AMAZING PERSON WITH INCREDIBLE TALENT, DRIVE AND PASSION. I AM NOT SURPRISED IN THE LEAST!"

Of course neither they nor the audience is expecting that size of a response from me, and at first are surprised, but quickly amused. After my rant, I explain that I want them to feel the power of that accomplishment in their cells. Most of us have lived not really celebrating anything other than big events like birthdays, graduations and promotions, so our brains are not being conditioned to seek success. We get in the habit of discounting what should be celebrated.

The rest of the assignment is then revealed. As they mingle and listen to the success stories, their job is to go crazy with celebration. Their response is to be as over the top as possible, causing the speaker to really feel the magnitude of that success. I literally want the speaker's body to shake do to the celebration they are experiencing.

In truth, it's a very emotional exercise. Most people are not comfortable with receiving praise and celebration. Sometimes, the participants are brought to tears because their minds simply don't know how to process someone telling them how great they are, especially at such an excited level.

Do I get a kick out of yelling at people? No. I want their minds to set a new mental bar when it comes to how they should feel when they accomplish something. Will they now go around asking people to scream in celebration at them when they do something as simple as the laundry? Most likely not. My belief, however, is that they will take just a little of that celebratory feeling and like it enough to not overlook the accomplishments and successes in their lives that they typically would have before.

I try to help break the habit of thinking of our lives and the "common" accomplishments we all make as normal and get people to create the habit of celebrating success.

Exercise: *Find Your Successes*

Take a moment and write down 10 successes in your life. Although you might not have people around you willing to scream at the top of their lungs about how awesome you are, when you are finished, read them out loud and give yourself a pat on the back... or at the very least a cool fist pump.

Find a more detailed exercise at www.thepracticecure.com

1. _____
2. _____
3. _____
4. _____
5. _____
6. _____
7. _____
8. _____
9. _____
10. _____

The value of recognizing and awarding success obviously has powerful psychological effects as well as tangible, real world results. As a manager, recognizing and awarding success is a key tool to creating more success for yourself personally, your staff, and your organization.

Implementing Celebrations

Now that you understand the value of celebrating success, it's important to know how to implement that culture of celebrating success in your practice. When the habit is created, your team will grow a stronger bond with one another, they will find new and unique ways to celebrate and support one another. You will hit goals you never thought were possible.

This attitude will spill over to your clients as well. Remember the way CTO celebrated a patient when he or she made the decision to get braces, and when a patient had them taken off? It was a little mini-party.

Remember the Day of Awesomeness? After my client implemented it in his office and posted it on Facebook, people started driving to see him (from up to three hours away) so that they could be a part of the celebration. Their clients want to celebrate with them, even if they had nothing to do with the success.

Success becomes infectious. When you find new, unique and frequent ways to celebrate success with your team, you will create a cascade of success in your office.

Celebrating Successfully

In order for the "success cascade" to fully take hold, the members of your team have to feel that the recognition and success they are receiving is genuine. If it is insincere or meaningless, anything you do could actually backfire and undermine your efforts. Employees might feel used, unenthusiastic, and resentful.

Here are the keys to celebrating successfully:

- **Successful recognition is specific.** You must identify the actual accomplishment or achievement.

- **Successful recognition is sincere.** Half-hearted, low-energy celebrations or acknowledgement can be detrimental.

- **Successful celebrations happen consistently.** If you celebrate the achievement of a goal or accomplishment for one person, or one step in a process, you MUST recognize and celebrate all of them.

Avoid using the phrase "Good Job", as sufficient recognition. Instead, clearly communicate what specifically was good about the job they did and how that accomplishment contributed to the big picture, and how it made you feel. As we discussed, gift cards and special bonuses are great, but more importantly thoughtful recognition of accomplishment and contribution contribute to feelings of success.

Additionally, don't forget to include everyone in the celebration. According to *Gallup Business Journal*, supervisors aren't the only ones employees want to receive positive recognition from — workers want to hear from their peers as well (thus the Success Squad example earlier). Once you as a leader start to model how to successfully celebrate employee accomplishments in a meaningful way, other team members will follow your lead. This is extremely valuable because coworkers often know each other well and spend more time with each other than with their manager. Therefore, coworkers are usually able to identify when celebrations are in order and when a peer has really done something excellent. Peer-to-peer praise is a great way to create a thriving, innovative and productive business.

Hopefully, by now you're convinced of the value behind celebrating success in your practice and why you need to make it a specific habit, not a random, fleeting idea. However, if you do need more convincing, here are seven reasons to celebrate:

1. A celebration along the way is a reminder of why you set the goal in the first place. Take the time to recognize what went well in achieving a goal. This will help reinforce positive behaviors and demonstrate to team members what is required to accomplish goals in order to celebrate again!

2. Recognition of a goal obtained substantially helps team bonding. Your team will unify around a bigger goal when you celebrate the achievement of intermediate goals.

3. Celebrating the success of those you work with, be they clients, customers or suppliers, will all help to build a sense of camaraderie.

4. Changing your team's mindset from "work" to "celebration" improves energy levels.

5. Human nature dictates that people want to work in winning teams. Celebrating success reminds people that their workplace has a winning team.

6. Employees who feel appreciated are more likely to remain engaged and produce high-quality work. A work celebration is a great way of showing your appreciation towards them.

7. Celebrating success is a low-hanging fruit in relation to employee engagement and employee recognition. Simply stated... this is one of those "Easy Implementation/High Impact activities" we've discussed in the past.

In the end, the real question is why would you not want to create a culture of celebrating success? It's not just fun; it's a proven method of earning more of it. And when it comes to getting more success, I can only believe you have gotten to this point in this book because you are someone who wants it.

Chapter Takeaway:

• Success is a system and is infectious. When you find new, unique and frequent ways to celebrate success with your team, you will create a cascade of success in your office.

• To celebrate successes successfully, the celebrations must be specific, sincere and consistent.

• Always be on the lookout for new reasons to celebrate.

"Setting an example is a choice. I have challenges as much as everybody does, but nobody knows. My decision was that when I come in that office, my team doesn't deserve a jerk, and neither do my patients. I can't be grumpy. I refuse to participate in that type of personality.

Can you just decide to have a good day? Yes. It's just a choice to say, "I'm going to feel better, I'm going to be better, I'm going to be nicer, I'm going to be positive, I'm going to not let anybody else have bad days." I demand it. You've come to work, so there is no drama. When you hit that door, you are on your A game. If I'm not following that myself, that's not cool.

The team wants to follow the guy that knows where he's going and has that vision. When I was the guy that just kind of went to work and it was a great means to an end, I wasn't a great leader.

Twenty years later, I decided we were going to be best in Ohio. That's a bigger dream and that's something that people can follow.

Now, they are excited about it."

Dr. Clarke Sanders, DDS
Stonecreek Dental

CONCLUSION

● ●

"Every ending is a new beginning. Through the grace of God, we can always start again."

— *Marianne Williamson*

Using the lesson in the last chapter, let me celebrate your success in reading this book. I want to thank you for taking the time in reading my thoughts and taking into consideration how these ideas can help you in your business.

I've attempted to follow the advice of author and architect Buckminster Fuller. Not trying to "change things by fighting the existing reality" but to create change by "building a new model that makes the existing model obsolete."

The existing model of not taking the time to educate our doctors, dentists and other professionals on the needs of practice ownership, business management, employee engagement and life balance does not serve the world we live in today. There must be a better way to help those who have dedicated their lives to the health and well being of our communities. They deserve it as professionals trying to serve, and we the community deserve it as we put our trust in their hands.

I hope through the pages in this book I was able to build a relationship with you — one that will serve you as you grow as a business owner and serve as a practitioner.

In the end I hope this information has opened you up to new ideas, giving you new focus on the importance of and how to strengthen your relationships.

That vision I asked you to create is attainable. It can be yours.

ABOUT THE AUTHOR

Since 2008, Award-winning mentor, trainer, speaker and body language expert, Dino Watt, The Relationship Expert has been helping high-income producers by replicating their business success into their personal relationships. His systems have been proven to create more happiness in marriages, more peace in the work place, more freedom from the many stresses in life and more revenue in your business.

As the owner of Our Ripple Effect, Inc., Dino has been privileged to travel the country helping people understand when they strengthen their relationships they will gain more of what they want in all areas of their life. From communications skills, marketing strategies, body language techniques and expert positioning, Dino spends his time first getting to know what your needs are and then creates a simple, effective way of delivering the results.

To help practice owners finally get the business education formal education failed to deliver, Dino has taken his unique style of teaching and transformed it into the written word with *The Practice Rx*. His simple and effective formula will help any business owner become a more effective leader, build a winning team, create more profit and create a culture of lasting success.

As a proud father of three and a husband to his childhood sweetheart for over 20 years, Dino is happiest to describe himself as a PHD - Proud Husband and Dad.

TAKE ADVANTAGE OF YOUR FREE
DISCOVERY SESSION
WITH DINO TODAY!

STEP 1: Fill out the application found at:
dinowatt.com/application

STEP 2: Schedule your complementary discovery session and find out how to apply principles from The Practice Rx directly in your business, with your unique circumstances.

NO OBLIGATION
TO PURCHASE!

Made in the USA
San Bernardino, CA
19 January 2020